THE RIDING HORSE REPAIR MANUAL

Not the Horse You Want?
Create Him from What You Have

Doug Payne

Forewords by Anne Kursinski & Linda Zang

TRAFALGAR SQUARE
North Pomfret, Vermont

This book is dedicated to the countless horses
whose genuine, tireless efforts allow us to join them
in the endless pursuit of excellence in sport.

First published in 2014 by
Trafalgar Square Books
North Pomfret, Vermont 05053

Printed in China

Library of Congress Cataloging-in-Publication Data
Payne, Doug, 1981-
  The riding horse repair manual : not the horse you want? create him from what you have / Doug Payne.
     pages cm
  Includes index.
  ISBN 978-1-57076-517-9
  1. Horses--Training. 2. Horses--Behavior. I. Title.
  SF287.P39 2013
  636.1'0835--dc23
                              2013009934

All photographs by Amy Katherine Dragoo (akdragoophoto.com) except: Intro 1, 2, 3 A–C, 4 A & B, 5 A & B, 6, III.4 A–C, III.5 A–C, III.13, III.25 A, III.28 B & C, III.30 A, III.35 C (Courtesy of Doug Payne); 4.4 A–H, III.14 A–F, III.32, III.33 A–R, III.34 A–F, III.35 D (Amy Young); III.24 B, III.25 B, III.28 A, III.29, III.30 B, III.35 A & B, III.36 (Shannon Brinkman/shannonbrinkman.zenfolio.com); III.24 A, III.31 (Richard Payne); III.26 (GRC Photography)

Diagrams and book design by Lauryl Eddlemon
Cover design by RM Didier
Typefaces: Avenir, Eagle

10 9 8 7 6 5 4 3 2 1

contents

Contents

FOREWORD BY
Anne Kursinski

I like to say there are no magic tricks to good riding. I learned this not only through years of experience in the saddle, but by listening to and learning from three great teachers of horsemanship: Jimmy Williams, Hilda Gurney, and George Morris. They taught me, and I have since repeatedly told others, that fine riding and great performances with an equine partner come only from hard work, discipline, practice, and a love of the horse.

And so, I feel I must firmly state that Doug Payne is not a miracle worker. He does not possess a magic wand that he waves to instantly transform a spoiled horse into an angelic one. However, he is an excellent and astute horseman with terrific feel who possesses a solid foundation in the basics acquired from—yes, you guessed it—*hard work, discipline, practice, and a love of the horse.* And therefore, he often achieves great performances with horses when other riders could not and succeeds with horses that other riders haven't been able to figure out.

Because Doug is not a *miracle worker*, but simply an educated and experienced rider *who knows what works*, the methods to his success can just as easily be ours to learn and use. In this book, *The Riding Horse Repair Manual*, Doug provides tips and explains his own techniques to find sensible solutions to common training and behavior problems under saddle. He walks us through what goes wrong, *why* it goes wrong, and then discusses intelligent ways we can go about finding a way forward (even when the horse insists on going every other way but forward!) He covers contact issues, "unruly outbursts," and jumping matters, to boot—there are a lot of great answers to tough training questions here.

There is nothing like watching and feeling horses learn, develop, and change—physically, mentally, and emotionally. I get tremendous pleasure from producing great horses, and when you see Doug competing with one of his "project" horses, you know that he does, too.

I hope that what you learn from these pages enables you to find a positive, happy rhythm with your own equine partner, whatever your discipline and pursuits.

Anne Kursinski

Five-Time Olympian and Author of *Anne Kursinski's Riding & Jumping Clinic: A Step-by-Step Course for Winning in the Hunter and Jumper Rings*

FOREWORD BY
Linda Zang

Doug Payne and I both count the Pony Club as a formative part of our evolution as horse people. The Pony Club is one of the finest international organizations I have come in contact with. It helps promote better horse care and riding basics, and brings together those who share a common love for the horse and desire to excel.

Doug and I also both sampled a variety of equestrian activities in our early years before focusing on any specific one. I tried Western, hunters, and eventing before eventually settling on dressage in my twenties. Doug, the product of a prominently horsey family, participated in the full spectrum of disciplines, including less common choices such as tetrathlon (which combines marksmanship and riding) and vaulting (gymnastics on horseback) before becoming best known as a talented young rider in competitive eventing circles.

Why does this history matter when considering Doug's book *The Riding Horse Repair Manual?* Firstly, I can attest that there is no better beginning for a rider than having lots of different horses in the backyard (to learn on and to learn from). By virtue of having horses to ride every day for most of the upright hours of his life, Doug has accumulated a rich and varied experience—his is a solid, no-nonsense foundation comprised of work ethic, respect for the horse, understanding of equine psychology, a secure and confident seat, and a toolbox of schooling exercises for correct work under saddle. Add to this an uncommon ability to stick with, click with, and "fix" the horses that others may have given up on, and you have a talented individual who has cultivated valuable know-how worthy of our attention.

It isn't often, whatever the equestrian circles you travel, that you meet someone who has never had a so-called "problem" horse—perhaps labeled "rank," "stubborn," "spoiled," "ruined," or "useless." Such descriptions arise so often because the horse world is filled with complicated animals that are expected to perform complicated feats of athleticism, sometimes in the hands of individuals with little experience or confidence in the saddle. Doug has a reputation for finding the way forward with horses that have proven "complex" on any number of levels, and it is how he proceeds with new "problem horses" and the issues they bring to the ring that he details in the pages of this book.

It really doesn't matter what kind of horse you own or what kind of horse you plan to buy. It doesn't matter if you ride dressage or dream of becoming a top show jumper. The reality of riding is that someday, one day, you'll have a horse that stumps you—he won't go forward; won't accept contact; or he rears, bucks, spins, or ducks out. When that day comes, you'll want Doug's advice on hand; you'll need his tips and tricks and exercises. It will save you time and money, and it may help you see that your "problem horse" isn't a "problem" at all—just a challenge worth meeting.

Best of luck in your riding and training endeavors.

Linda Zang

FEI "O" Dressage Judge
Roemer Foundation/USDF Hall of Fame Inductee

PART I
Getting Started

···➤

introduction

How did I become the rider to turn to when people encountered a bump in the road—or even an entire roadblock—in their training? I was born into a very involved horse family. My mother maintains a bustling training, judging and lesson business in Oldwick, New Jersey. She has become one of the top dressage judges in the world, judging eventing at the Olympic Games in 2008, the 2010 World Equestrian Games, and every eventing CCI**** in the world. During our time growing up, there were countless horses passing through the farm and riders were always needed.

My sister Holly and I had one horse of our own and rode whatever else we could get our hands on until the time came to head off to college. Both of us were products of our local Pony Club, both graduated as A's. During the years in Pony Club we took part in nearly every discipline offered, as well as a few related competitions that were not under the Pony Club's direction. Outside the normal dressage, jumping and eventing we grew up with, every year we rode in competitive games, Tetrathlon and partook in the Pony Club's Know-Down Classroom (known today as the Quiz). We also rode in the Far Hills, New Jersey, pony races.

One of the most valuable things we ever did with horses was vaulting. I can't recommend it enough for children growing up. Vaulting is gymnastics on horseback; it improves a participant's balance, agility and coordination, but most importantly, it teaches you how to fall. It's just a fact of life that if you plan to ride for a long period of time, you're going to fall. Learning to fall correctly will greatly improve your ability to land and roll away unscathed.

I heard about an instructor who lined up all the children at their first ever riding lesson. This entire lesson just consisted of each child mounting a pony and being pushed off into the dirt. Every child started with a lot of reservations—and nervousness—but soon enough they were basically throwing themselves off the pony. The more they fell, the more comfortable they became. Their natural apprehension was gone, as too was the most common inhibition when learning to ride—fear.

We were lucky to get a lot more practice falling off than most by riding bareback for most of the time in our youth. I was not a fan in the least of cleaning tack, so why make it dirty? I didn't consistently use a saddle until I was in my mid-teens. One of my sister's and my favorite games with our pony was to gallop her as fast as we could in a field. Then we'd drop the reins and she would instantly slam on the brakes and drop her head for grass. We'd slide down her

1 I'm just getting on our first pony named Popcorn. Holding her is my mom, and my sister is walking away with Patches.

2 This old photo was taken at my family's annual Christmas gymkhana in the high jump competition. Needless to say, I did not win!

neck landing on the grass in front of her then vault back on, and repeat the process. There was no limit to what we'd do bareback, from flatwork to jumping and cross-country. This was not just over small jumps—at the time, the horse I was riding was competing through Preliminary in eventing. All of our preparation for the weekend's event was completed saddle-free.

Neither my sister nor I can remember our first time on a horse, or for that matter, our first show. We were blessed to grow up fully entrenched in the equestrian world—it was just something you did growing up. We knew no different. By the time we reached our teens we were both heavily involved in the United States Equestrian Association (USEA) Young Rider program. New Jersey is located in Area II where we were coached by the legendary Jimmy Wofford. His program and style was excellent for all of us, engaging and structured, as only Jimmy can pull off. Of the original group who participated in these annual training camps at Gladstone, no fewer than ten of us have continued on to become professionals competing at the top levels of our sport today. I find myself, almost daily, referring to the foundation he instilled in us years ago.

My sister was very lucky in that her first horse after ponies happened to develop into a very successful eventer. She took The Federalist all the way from Novice through the Advanced level, and in 2000, they placed fourth at the North American Young Rider Championships and earned a Team Gold Medal. At the time, Holly's success was a rather bitter pill for me to swallow. To say our family is competitive is an understatement! Just about any monotonous activity became anything but—it quickly turned into a cutthroat game. Losing wasn't an option. To give you an example: On the average afternoon my sister and I would return from school and have a contest starting at the door going out of the house. The rules were simple—the winner was the one who could catch a turned-out horse, tack up and be first mounted. It was common for us to challenge each other in all sorts of jumping contests—different lines, heights, long-spot or short-spot contests. Just about anything you could imagine was turned into a game.

During those years I didn't have a consistent horse that stayed sound enough, was talented enough, or wasn't sold by his owner. While extremely frustrating at the time, I always had time to ride the "new" horse at the barn. Regardless of what mental quirk or training issue he had, I was determined to figure him out as best as I could. I wanted to get back in the game to beat my

3 A-C Here, I'm riding Just a Star at the 2001 NAYRC (North American Young Riders Competition) in Parker, Colorado. I'm just about to jump into the water on the cross-country phase of the eventing competition (A); in the show jumping phase (B); and in the Awards Ceremony, where I'm accepting the Silver Medal.

sister. Every horse that stepped foot on the property had the potential to be my ticket—I just needed to figure out how to ride him well. Another advantage of growing up in such a rich, performance-horse environment was that it wasn't just event horses coming through the barn, it was anything from dressage horses, to jumpers, fox hunters, show hunters, or simply pleasure horses. This diversity in discipline, breed, focus, sales, and training gave me an incredible opportunity to develop the skills needed to get the most out of each horse in a timely fashion. Frankly, if I hadn't been able to figure a horse out quickly, I wouldn't have ridden him for much longer!

By the age of 18, I had competed countless horses, the most successful of which had allowed me to compete at the North American Young Rider Championships (NAYRC) CCI** level for Area II as well my first Advanced event. Aside from the eventing, I was actively competing in dressage and had ridden through Prix St. George on three horses.

I was also very involved in Tetrathlon through the U.S. Pony Club. Tetrathlon is a sport that combines riding (show jumping in the United States and cross-country in the United Kingdom), running, swimming and pistol shooting. I was the US national champion and a member of two international teams that I joined on a tour of England and Ireland for nearly a month at a time. This was my first taste of competing overseas. Representing your country is like a drug; once you get a taste, you can't get enough. You're more driven than ever to get there again.

The deal struck with our parents growing up was that they would provide a horse for us to ride and compete through high school; upon graduating, we had to sell whatever horse we had at the time, regardless of his level or success. College was a must, and any horse activities from that point on were solely on our dime. Again, we were lucky that we'd already had an introduction to professional riding as it helped put us through college. During school, I managed to scrape together enough money to purchase a horse from Ireland named Cornerhouse. He was green broke, but a few years later he went on to win the American Eventing Championships. I sold him for the down payment on my apartment in Gladstone just following his first CCI** at Radnor, Pennsylvania.

My education was capped off at the Rochester Institute of Technology where I graduated with a degree in Mechanical Engineering. Funny thing was that I had no intention of continuing—at that point—as a professional equestrian. Little did I realize it at the time but the engineering program laid the foundation for my success with horses. Following the Institute's five-year program, graduates come out of the rigorous engineering course

4 A & B In A, I'm participating in the riding phase of the 2001 USPC (Pony Club) International Tetrathlon Exchange held at High Prairie Farms Equestrian Center in Colorado. In B you see the shooting phase—I'm wearing the orange hat (B).

with a very solid, black-and-white analytical approach to problem-solving. It becomes second nature to analyze each problem without allowing emotion to impact your decision. This is vitally important when training horses: In many ways, horses are not complex creatures, as much as we'd like to personify them.

Many would wonder why I didn't see myself riding for the rest of my life, but the lifestyle of a professional trainer was not appealing to me. I had lived the life as a child and couldn't see myself teaching from seven o'clock in the morning to eight o'clock at night every day as my mother did dur-

5 A & B

Photo A was taken in Ireland the day I purchased Cornerhouse, sarcastically nicknamed "Killer" because of his "puppy-dog" personality! Two years later, Photo B shows Killer at the 2005 American Eventing Championships, held at Five Points Horse Park in Raeford, North Carolina, where he won the Preliminary Division. This was my first national title in eventing.

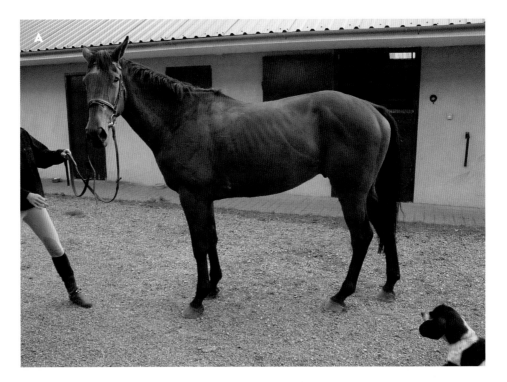

ing her time between judging jobs. I preferred just working with horses, trying to figure out what made them tick, and how I could best form a partnership with them to succeed as a team. I didn't realize that I could make a living doing just that!

I fully intended to get into the field of Forensic Engineering and ride horses on the side, and I was about a year into the

application to become a state police officer with the intention of working in the forensic investigation unit. I had worked as an intern for a forensic engineer during my time at RIT. The plan was to gain sufficient experience with the state police in order to go off on my own as an expert consultant. I figured I'd split my time consulting and riding.

Well long story short, the state went bankrupt and the start date for the academy was pushed back further with each passing week. During that year of uncertainty, I continued riding and training—more and more. The average day involved traveling around to different farms to ride all sorts of horses, from bucking Quarter Horses to rearing Warmblood crosses to Appaloosas with attitudes. You can imagine that list is endless!

I was riding roughly 10 horses a day and making very close to the starting salary of a state police officer. And, there was another consideration that changed the course of my life. What I hadn't taken into consideration was the fact that if I rode for a living, my horses would become a business expense. So I figured if I didn't take the opportunity, I would regret not trying it by the time I hit 35. I can't tell you how happy I am now that I made that choice!

The business began in earnest. I rented a barn and hung up my sign. Within the first year, I had the barn full of horses demonstrating every conceivable issue you could imagine. Most problems I'd seen before, but of course, there were some more interesting than others.

Every day brought something new to the table. The more the horse was athletic and intelligent, the bigger the challenge, though more rewarding in the end. Out of the "orangutans" grew a few exceptional athletes that could take me to the top of the sport. My goal has always been to reach the top of not just eventing, but the individual Olympic disciplines of show jumping and dressage, as well.

The first few years in business brought a constant stream of horses, usually for some sort of "behavior boot camp." On average, they'd stay from one to three months. We had roughly 12 horses at a time. As time passed, the average talent level increased, as did the duration of their stay. I've been lucky enough to find a few diamonds in the rough.

Riding this wide gamut of horses that entered the farm was the best thing that could have happened to me. Horses are your best instructor. If you are lucky enough to ride a number of them on a consistent basis you begin to see trends: When you see a problem develop in one horse it can be discounted as a flaw in that horse, but when that problem arrives in more than one, you had better be looking in the mirror for the reason behind it. It's you! Oftentimes, realizing and acting on this is difficult, but it's the only way you'll truly improve enough to achieve your dreams.

A Learning Experience

The most interesting duo ever to step in the barn, both owned by Susan and Dave Drillock, were Alf, a Fjord, and Billy, a PMU rescue. This first story is about Alf. Despite one of the cutest faces known to man, he had a tremendous bucking habit, and Susan, who happens to be the kindest, most caring person I've met, did not appreciate hitting the dirt! While I had dealt with many bucking horses in the past, staying on him was more of a challenge. Compounding his athleticism was the fact that he was just about as wide as tall, with no withers to speak of. One of the first days at the farm, he was giving his best impression of a bronco, added a turn, and around his barrel went my saddle—and I very soon followed suit. I have to admit that I am known for having a girth on the looser side, but from that point on, Alf struggled to breathe! Unfortunately, I did hit the dirt a number of times as my saddle continued to slip around his barrel—I always wished a set of withers could be developed to put on him!

Upon their arrival neither Alf nor Billy had been shown; the goal was to give them a solid foundation to build on, but overall, to work the kinks out so that they would be as safe as possible for Susan and Dave. While both solidly built, the two were quite different and needed to be treated as such. Alf was the more mischievous of the two: His bucking was more of a reluctance to work rather than

6 Billy and Alf.

genuine fear or misunderstanding. Ultimately, he could be dealt with directly.

Billy, on the other hand, was a much more sensitive type. He was genuinely scared and often acted out purely as a flight response to a threat. Alf progressed quickly: When he understood he'd be spanked for bucking, he stopped. Billy took a bit more time and patience, but as his experience grew and he understood that the world was not such a scary place, he began to grow into himself.

In the end, I was never able to get Alf's withers to pop up! However, both horses progressed along well, entering a few local shows and events. Billy is still being ridden and occasionally shown by friends of the Drillocks. Susan has taken up driving and luckily Alf has been able to put his solid flatwork foundation to good use in this new activity.

So where do I sit today? I have a thriving training and competition business. We have roughly 15 to 20 horses at the farm: from Beginner Novice to Advanced eventers, Level 0 to Grand Prix show jumpers, and up to Fourth-Level dressage horses.

Outside riding, I am a United States Eventing Association (USEA) certified instructor as well as a United States Equestrian Federation (USEF) judge and Technical Delegate. I've found their training programs invaluable, not only for their intended use, but also in the show ring as a competitor. The USEF Event Judges program, in particular, has done wonders for me in many ways. Naively, I had no idea that the program would transform how I looked at my riding and training. I had grown up with one of the best judges in the world and figured I knew most of what there was to be taught. But, I couldn't have been more wrong. The program explicitly covers all aspects of not only judging but also training of horses. It's helped me immensely day to day, as well as in the ring while showing.

Through the hundreds of horses I've ridden to this point, I have a unique advantage that allows me to get the most out of a horse and allow him to develop to his full potential. I also have gathered the experience necessary for dealing with whatever behavior problems and training issues are "thrown" at me and can "reclaim" perfectly good horses for riding and competition through rehabilitation.

chapter one

A Strategy for Avoiding
Behavior Problems

All riders begin their journey in equestrian sports for a multitude of different reasons, with the common thread across disciplines being that they'd like to have a cooperative and happy horse that continues to progress. After all, a happy horse generally means a happy rider. However, there are many horses out there that are not "happy." Known as "problem horses" they can exhibit numerous behaviors that are not conducive to producing an enjoyable—or, in some cases, even safe—ride. Many times, these behaviors have their root in poor riding and training. Nearly always, such problems can be fixed with correct riding and retraining so these horses can be "reclaimed," and enjoy their intended job.

It is my intention in this book to provide you with the rider tools necessary for rehabilitating all manner of horses. These problems can be as simple as a lazy partner or as dramatic as a rearing horse that is dead set on leaving you in the dust. There is a light at the end of the tunnel; this book will be your guide through the dark!

In Part One, I'll briefly discuss my training program, from how to start a green horse through work on the ground, mounting for the first time, longeing, and ridden work. I then assess behavior problems, the reasons they occur, and tell you how to evaluate your own horse.

In Part Two, I first ask you to evaluate yourself as a rider, then I get to the challenging business of solving the common riding problems that most riders can successfully manage to overcome. This part is divided into three sections—Section I: Contact Issues (p. 65); Section II: Unruly Outbursts (p. 91); and Section III: Jumping Problems (p. 133). For all the individual issues that I outline, I explain the possible causes, as well as offer you tips and solutions—sometimes many different ones—to each problem. In Part Three, I'll give you strategies to ensure your future success—both with the horse you may have now, and those you might ride in the future.

Now, before I outline my training program I want to discuss the importance of the rider. Two of the biggest roadblocks to becoming an accomplished rider are 1) not being objective about your skill set, and 2) failing (or not wanting) to recognize that the learning process with horses is neverending. Horses are about the most honest creatures you'll find, and they can see a "fake" without fail. As a rider, and student of the sport, you should be objective and honest with yourself (and upfront with your instructor). Being honest about your riding will get you much farther—and faster—than trying to shortcut your way to the top. In any event, your shortcomings will be evident through the actions of your horse, so find your weaknesses, and fix them.

In the ideal world a novice rider would be taught on a "schoolmaster," and over time, as her competence increased, she would be able to ride greener and greener horses. Although a very common practice today, it is extremely difficult for a green rider to ride and train a green horse. The more experienced horse, with a correctly applied aid, will most often give the desired result, and he adds a positive feedback loop, which greatly increases the speed at which the rider can develop. In a green partnership, however, a rider may ask correctly, but unless the horse responds as he should, which may or may not happen due to ignorance or uncertainty, the rider will not have the confidence that she asked correctly and she'll try another aid, oftentimes sending the horse in the wrong direction.

Get Help

Throughout your journey with horses I can't overstate how important it is to obtain the best instruction you can manage to find. It's very easy to get wrapped up in you-and-your-horse issues. However, a good teacher will be able to discern differences and point out small changes in your technique that will result in major improvements in your horse's performance.

Success should be measured by demonstrating a constant improving trend in your and your horse's relationship and performance. But, when you feel you have stagnated or regressed, it's time to get another set of eyes on the situation or vary your education in other ways.

How is this best done? There are limitless resources out there to help. You're taking a great step reading this book and there are many others out there that can also shed some light on a situation. I find clinics very helpful, especially once a solid foundation has been established, you can always learn from a clinician. You might not come away with a *revolutionary* change in your riding, but instead, an *evolutionary* one: Any

clinic or lesson should be considered successful when you learn one more concept, gain a new tool or a feeling that you can implement in future rides.

Take the time to travel to the top competitions of your riding discipline to watch. If this is not possible, utilize all the resources you can muster. Take advantage of YouTube and live feed broadcasts from international competitions. Studies have proven that a tennis fan's game improves just after watching a top tournament where the best in the world are playing. It will, without a doubt, open your eyes to what is possible. Also, it is human nature to mimic what is seen. It's very easy to ride daily at your barn with the same people; without fail, most fall into their barn's hierarchy and don't ever improve. Being the big fish in the little pond should not be your goal. Your pond is most likely a puddle, and there's an ocean out there! Ride with the best and you'll quickly raise your game. It should not be acceptable to be good when you're still miles from your personal potential. Make the most of all the time with your horse.

Problems in the ridden horse, the subject of this book, often have a multitude of contributing factors that result in all the symptoms—unwanted behavior—that I'll be discussing in detail in Part Two. These factors can be related to a horse's general well-being or his training. First, it's important to rule out the possibility that a physical issue is the reason your horse is exhibiting unwanted behaviors. However, I say this with some reservation. Although I fully recognize that injury, stiffness or general soreness can be the root of a problem, all too often people go on veterinary "witch hunts" looking for some cause of their riding issue when nine times out of ten, that problem is sitting on the horse's back!

There are plenty of companies in business today who thrive on their million different remedies for all of your horse's problems, which fit right in with the modern psyche where instant gratification is king. But, the majority of these supplements end up fertilizing your fields at best—a hell of an expensive way to grow greener grass if you ask me.

I do suggest, however, that you should get a basic veterinary exam completed to rule out any significant factors. Once this is done, however, put it out of your mind.

Once any significant medical problems are ruled out you have to remember that your horse has the "job of a lifetime." He will get a day or two or more off per week and on the days he does work, he'll have 23 hours off with the remaining one to get groomed, generally fussed over, and exercised. Otherwise, he just eats, sleeps and socializes. Not bad if you ask me!

With this in mind you should expect his attention and effort when you're working with him. Keep in mind every interaction—good, bad, or indifferent—you have with your horse, regardless if you realize it or not, is actually *training* him. You're training him every moment!

Lay a Solid Foundation

It's my experience that most behavioral problems are the result of steps in the horse's training that have not been sufficiently covered or understood by him. When training horses, you have to be methodical in your approach. Each day you must review concepts from the past as well as the new concepts you covered the previous day. When they are easily performed, the next step can be introduced.

It is very easy to get ahead of yourself. When your horse has difficulty with anything you present him, you must break it down to its most basic components. Like the salesman's motto, an answer of "no" is *never* a "no"; you just haven't asked the question in the correct way. Ask again—just figure out a different way to phrase it this time.

Every day your job is to instill a new and elevated level of confidence. If your horse could talk, he should be able to describe exactly what he learned that day. Since that's impossible, look for unspoken signs that you've been successful: Your horse should be calmer and more "in tune" with you when you finish than when you started. He should have an air of quiet confidence about him, as if he wished all of his friends could see him at work.

Your "theme" of the day should be presented in a number of different ways so that your horse has the best opportunity to understand what you are after. You are looking for him to be able to perform whatever you ask better than he's ever been able to before. There will be some days when you'll feel as if his training has regressed. When this is the case, you probably are presenting new information faster than he can process it. So, break it down into smaller chunks, and achieve them. You'll end up progressing much faster than the rider who simply pushes through while ignoring any warning signs. Horses progress at their own rate. If you push them beyond their comfort level they'll find a way to slow it down. This is most often seen when people over-face their horse while jumping; when this happens, the horse will "shut down," and you'll spend an extraordinary amount of time undoing shortcuts, fixing the damage.

When you are confident you've laid a solid foundation, each day you can push the envelope. Again, not so much so that your horse can't comprehend and execute what is being asked. However, horses will generally rise to the occasion so push the boundaries, and don't be surprised when your horse surpasses your expectations.

It's important to keep in mind competitive success will follow solid training. You goal should not be to win each competition you enter; instead you can use some to teach your horse as much as possible in order to give him the experience and training needed to win. Results will follow, without a doubt.

chapter two

How to Start a Green Horse:
A Brief Guide

The Appropriate Use of Aids

As a horseman, you have access to *natural* and *artificial* aids. *Natural* are your seat, leg, voice, weight and hands, while *artificial* are the whip and spurs. Always look to use more refined natural aids that will eventually be invisible to an observer. Don't expect this to happen overnight; you'll be working to improve these for a lifetime. In time, your goal is to accomplish nearly everything in riding just with your seat, balance, leg and hand.

With few exceptions, I use both spurs and a whip every time I ride to refine the tools I was born with. They should not be used for every cue or even close, but when needed, they are an essential reinforcement, and if not attached to your boots or in your hand, you're out of luck. However, riders that have yet to establish solid basics should not use spurs; any inadvertent use of spurs or the whip due to lack of control or stability must be avoided. It is important in the training process that you are in full control of your aids. Inadvertent application will only confuse your horse and derail your progress.

Riding Positions and Aids

To explain the effectiveness and uses of riding positions and aids: As you travel from your hip to your ankle, your ability to make fine, precise movements decreases and the intensity of your aid becomes greater. It's effectively going from a very fine adjustment at your core down to a coarse one at your heel. You should aim to be able to ask your horse to walk, trot, canter and move laterally with just a small application of pressure from your seat and upper leg. So how do your whip and spurs fit in? In order to use them correctly, first use the natural aids. When an aid is given and the desired response is not seen, ask again with the same intensity, and, at the same time, use your spurs to reinforce your natural aid. If that doesn't work, use both spurs and whip. It's critical to keep in mind that your goal is to tune your horse to a point where subtle natural aids are all that are needed to perform even the most intricate movements. With a green horse, don't be afraid to be very clear and deliberate with your leg and hand. As your horse's training progresses you can start to use smaller, more refined aids and expect an identical response.

For example, with a very young or green horse, in order to make a 15-meter circle to the right, I use a clearly open rein on the inside, with my outside leg and rein on to bring his shoulder around. Now if I were to hop on a Grand Prix dressage horse, this same circle will be initiated with the smallest of squeezes with the outside rein, enough inside rein to keep the flexion, and a small application of outside thigh. The same result of circling to the right is achieved with about 1/100th of the aid I needed for the "baby."

Now, if that Grand Prix dressage horse had started to drift and I closed my fingers and thigh on the left—to no effect—I'd react quickly with a firm correction. With the baby, however, I would be happy to get close to the 15-meter circle and a drift

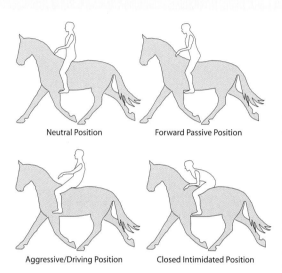

Neutral Position   Forward Passive Position

Aggressive/Driving Position   Closed Intimidated Position

Diagram 1 The four riding positions.

wouldn't be viewed as a big fault. I'll certainly attempt to correct it, but will be happy with a good effort on his part. If the circle ended up at 17 meters instead, no big deal. I'd just continue the circle until it was 15 meters round. You must have the goal of refinement in mind but be aware of what you're riding at the moment.

To summarize: Artificial aids should be used in concert with natural aids. Your aim is always to assist the horse in understanding what you're asking. In a normal situation, artificial aids are not used to punish your horse, just to educate.

I like to think of your body as a cohesive system with all pieces working together; while your body must be able to give independent aids when communicating, no component can be used without impacting another.

It is also important to realize just how much your seat and balance can affect your horse. A well-trained animal can be taught to perform nearly all movements from your seat and weight aids alone. This is your goal. The more subtle your aids become the greater you'll find freedom and relaxation in your horse; with more elasticity your horse will have the best chance of reaching his potential. Imagine that your center of gravity—just around your belly button—is the finest possible aid you can use; as your aids move farther away from your core toward your extremities, their severity increases while their refinement decreases.

A Training Timeline

Regarding a timeline, keep in mind that each horse progresses at a different rate, so no advice about timing can be set in stone. Your gut feeling will tell you a lot, and when in doubt remind yourself that there is no rush.

I think it might be helpful to cover how we start horses at our farm from the moment they arrive at the barn. For the purposes here, let's assume we have a weanling who has been "untouched." Regardless of his future discipline, breaking and initial training is the same; he won't start to specialize until he is in his five-year-old year. Even when he is picked to be a dressage horse down the road, we strive to keep his life interesting by exposing him to as many experiences as possible. All the horses will learn to trot and canter over ground poles. Later, we'll have a day or two during the week that we'll do a little jumping, or just take him for a ride outside the ring. It's important not to get into a routine where you just "pound" and, as a result, over-train and burn him out. This sort of training destroys any horse's willingness to improve. Soon enough, he'll be resentful of the ring, no longer coming out each day eager to learn.

Up until he is three, this weanling is handled on a daily basis. He will usually live outside 24 hours a day so he can be a "horse." This handling can be as simple as a quick once-over and brushing in the field to bringing him into the barn to have a more thorough cleaning. He will be brushed, clipped, have his feet picked out and his mane pulled—all just general interaction. We also like to introduce him to tack earlier rather than later, and may even "pony" him out on the trail.

Your intent should be to maintain an overall standard of health as well as make him comfortable and accept, or better yet, *look forward to* human interaction. From a young age, you want him to establish a healthy respect for people. It's easier and much safer to get the upper hand when he is 12 hands rather than the 17+ hands he'll be at three years and ready for you to get on for the first time.

Groundwork

By the fall of his three-year-old year when we generally begin the formal breaking process, he should be able to be lead without running you down. We begin to teach voice commands on the lead before moving forward. I expect him to be able to walk and halt on voice command.

How exactly is this groundwork done? I'll start with the necessary equipment. I use a halter with a chain lead over the bridle

2.1 A & B In A, Simon is modeling our basic set up, with a halter and chain on top, for his first few rides. This bridle happens to be a figure-eight. I have no problem if it's a regular noseband with a flash, or a drop noseband. He is wearing a double-jointed, full-cheek snaffle. In B, I am holding the lead rope with the reins wrapped and looped into the halter to prevent a rein from being caught in the horse's leg.

2.2 I'm ready to work Simon in hand.

(figs. 2.1 A & B and see p. 30 for introduction to the bridle). Some people like to use a Western-style rope halter, which is fine, too. Regardless, you need some way of gaining the upper hand should the horse try to run over you, or just when he's not being as responsive as you'd like. Using a generic halter with a plain cotton lead is *not* acceptable. Horses are not stupid, and when they figure out there is no consequence when they don't listen to you, you are in deep trouble!

I also use a dressage whip in my left hand as an additional driving aid when teaching voice commands. And, I strongly recommend the use of gloves! Nothing is worse than a horse that spooks or just plain decides that he'd rather be somewhere else so he bolts after ripping the lead line through your hands.

I like to train a horse to voice commands from the ground—first by leading him, then by longeing (fig. 2.2). Using side-reins, longeing progresses to walk, trot, and canter (see p. 34 for more about longeing). The horse should be able to perform all three gaits (as well as halt) from your voice commands alone. It's helpful to accentuate different portions of each word used to make it more clear to your horse what you are asking: *walk* (waaaaaallk), *trot* (trrrrrrrroot), *canter* (cannnnter) and *ho* or *whoa* (hooooo).

Later, when the rider is slowly introduced, physical aids—legs, seat and hand—can be taught with ease by using the voice as an association.

In Hand

In hand, I expect horses to be able to move forward, backward and sideways without hesitation.

The first step in the process is walking forward. When leading your young horse, stand on his left side, just in front of the shoulder. I can't stand leading a horse that expects you to literally "drag" him forward. It's his job to walk; you're just there to guide his direction.

The opposite is also not good: A horse that drags you along is simply dangerous. Remember, you are the dominant player in the partnership you're creating. If your horse sees you as a weak leader, he will try to take charge.

Expect to remain just in front of his shoulder at all times. Your right hand should be near the end of the chain where the leather or cotton portion is attached. Any slack along with your dressage whip should be held in your left hand. When using it, extend your *left* hand backward and rotate your wrist to lightly tap his hindquarters while maintaining control of his head.

*tip *The single most important quality in any horseman is a methodical approach to training where negative emotions have no place whatsoever. Bad temper will be counterproductive, I assure you. It takes time to gain a horse's trust, and when it is lost it can be an extraordinarily long process to attempt to recover it.*

Horses are very intuitive creatures. They are extremely perceptive to body language as well as their handler's inner confidence—or nervousness. It's easier said than done, but always try to remain calm and confident. The best horsemen I've ever met are at peace with themselves: Their horses tend to follow their lead, gaining confidence, not only in their leader, but in themselves, too.

CAUTION: Don't anthropomorphize! I feel this is one the most important pieces of advice I can offer. All too often, people tend to attach human traits to equine behavior. Horses are not high-level thinkers. By nature most are very genuine, trusting animals that are looking to please. Throughout the educational process, take a step back, don't overthink it. There is usually a very simple answer.

Treat the Horse as an Individual

It's vitally important to get a very good feel for each individual horse—all are different, some much more sensitive than others. You have to gauge how much pressure should be applied to garner the desired response. Some lighter breeds and types are very reactive. For instance, if you've just rescued a hot little Thoroughbred off the track, you've got a sensitive firecracker on your hands, where even the lightest aid will create an immediate, overreactive response. A horse like this requires a skilled handler who has an intuitive feel of how much is too much; the horse would not be an appropriate match to a beginner or novice rider who will not have the body control to prevent giving inadvertent cues.

On the other hand, when you happen to come upon a horse that is a "dead head," you might end up having to be quite firm to get any response! A request that hardly gets a twitch of an ear from the dead head might send the hot type through the roof!

In the infancy of your new horse's training, nip in the bud the "bully-type" behaviors. It's important for your safety to be firm with horses that don't respect your personal space. When leading or dealing with a horse, it's unacceptable for him to barge or run into or over you. When this happens, be quick and decisive in your corrections. Don't be afraid to be firm; it's for your safety, and if addressed early on, you won't have to worry about the horse later in life. You cannot be concerned about hurting your horse's feelings; you're not trying to be best friends. Horses have to respect and look up to you. This is the only way you'll develop a lasting bond. Your relationship needs someone to "wear the pants," so it had better be you!

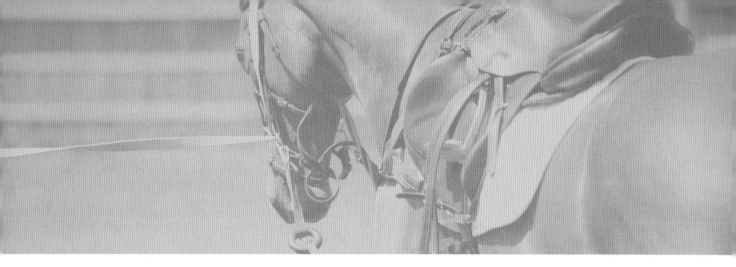

Training Step by Step:
Work on the Ground

In-Hand Training Methods

Your goal is to train every horse, regardless of his natural sensitivity, to pay close enough attention so that no perceptible input from you is needed. He should be paying close enough attention so when you begin to walk forward, he walks with you.

In order to better understand how to train your horse it's beneficial to understand by what means you communicate with him. For your purposes, I'd like to highlight three techniques we most frequently used with our horses. They are: negative reinforcement; positive reinforcement; and positive punishment.

Negative reinforcement should be the primary method used while riding, and it is the most important to understand: A stimulus is removed from your horse's experience in order to increase the likelihood of a behavior happening again. A most basic example: You apply pressure to your right rein and it remains until the horse yields and moves his head to the right. As soon as he does, you release the pressure. If

The whole concept of training: 1) Apply pressure 2) As soon as correct response is obtained, reward by releasing pressure.

consistently applied, you will have to use a smaller and smaller amount of pressure to achieve the same response. The very best riders in the world appear from a bystander not to be doing anything. This is your goal!

Positive reinforcement is where a stimulus is added to the horse's experience upon completion of a behavior.

Positive punishment is where an *adverse* stimulus is added to your horse's experience with the goal of reducing the frequency of a behavior. The most common example of positive punishment is using the whip to reinforce your leg aids. You are looking for your horse to respond by moving away from leg pressure. If he does not respond, you apply the whip until he moves off your leg, at which time the stimulus is removed.

Exercise

1 When asking your horse to walk forward, say "Walk" and speak clearly and confidently. At the same time you should begin to walk forward and give him a very light tap with your whip. Some will pick this up instantly, while others might take some more convincing. Quickly you'll get a feel of how much pressure is needed.

2 Once your horse is walking with you, the next step is to ask him to stop. Again, clearly and confidently say "Whoa" or "Ho." At the same time stop walking yourself, and a moment later give a light, quick tug on the lead. If this doesn't get the desired response, repeat with a stronger aid until your horse stops.

> **tip** *I make sure to have some treats with me at all times. Most horses love sugar. Cubes are easy to find and easy to use, but you can also use carrots, grain or any other treat that will get his attention. (However, like anything else, too much of a good thing can be counterproductive; you want to make sure you don't produce a spoiled horse.)*

3 Once you can walk forward and stop without trouble, the next step is to teach your horse to back up and move sideways (fig. 3.1). You teach your horse to go back from the halt. Before asking, begin by stepping in front of your horse. I prefer to switch hands so that the left is closest to the halter, giving me the freedom to use my right hand to guide him. Apply light pressure on the lead, and at the same time, use your right hand to gently press on his chest. Once he takes a step back, reward him by quickly removing the aid. Remember, if the initial aid does not have the desired result, simply gradually increase it until you see a response. Don't go for broke: If you get one step back, soften and ask again.

4 At the point when he will back up with confidence, with no limit to the number of steps, teach him to do the same while you stand next to his shoulder in the conventional leading position. The same method can be used—a light pressure or tug—but, in addition, you can use your right elbow to make contact with his chest. The association should be clear to the horse at this point.

5 Now it is time to to teach your horse to move laterally. Stand on his right side with the lead in your left hand, and gently press on his barrel with your right hand at roughly the area where your leg will be when mounted (figs. 3.2 A & B). At first, your horse might attempt to move forward to release the pressure. Should this happen, give another tug

3.1 Here, I am teaching Simon to back up with pressure applied to the lead as well as his chest. The moment he takes a step back, I reward him by releasing the pressure.

on the lead to make it clear you don't want him to move forward. At the same time, apply some lateral pressure to create some bend in his neck. The bend will naturally make the horse want to move his haunches in the opposite direction.

Repeat this process until your horse steps sideways. When your hand is placed at his side, he should yield away from it and be rewarded by the release of the pressure. This concept is introduced on the ground and will be

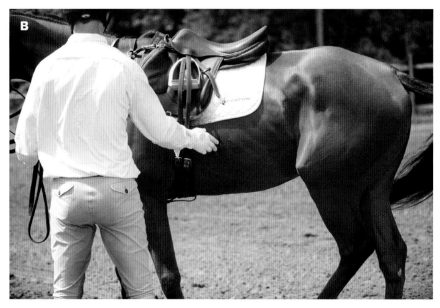

3.2 A & B Both of these photos show the beginning of the association and yielding from pressure while maintaining contact with the lead. I'm applying pressure with my right hand where my leg will be once I'm mounted. Appropriately, Simon steps to his right with his hind end, and I quickly release the pressure and give him a pat as a reward.

used when mounted on your horse for the rest of his life. You're laying the foundation for a means of nonverbal communication.

Introducing Tack

Once you are able to move your horse left, right, forward and back, you can move on to prepare him for longeing (see p. 34). Before I get there, I like to introduce all the tack that will be required later for riding.

Bridle

I like to use a double-jointed full cheek snaffle bit on a simple bridle with a flash noseband on the young horses. This bit has a very forgiving mouthpiece, and the full cheek also gives you more lateral support to make turning much easier. That said, your first few rides will feel as if you're steering a barge through a canal. Unintended collisions are quite likely!

1 Introduce the bridle with a treat in hand. The first few times will be on the cross-ties or in a stall. Gently place the bridle on so that he gets the treat at the same time he takes the bit. A positive association is your goal—especially the first few times. The introduction of a bridle should take a few days. The first day, your goal should be to get the bridle on and leave it for a few minutes, working up to longer periods over the following week.

2 The next step is to introduce the action of the bit. Apply a small amount of downward pressure to the reins, at the same time putting light pressure on the poll. The moment your horse yields—that is, his head drops down—reward him

---

The Cold-Backed Horse

How do you identify a cold backed horse? Like other specific issues, the severity of this condition varies.

When starting any horse you don't know well, be very aware as you introduce the saddle pad, saddle and girth. Even later in a horse's life, I am always careful as I tighten a girth to look for him to become slightly more tense or "hump" his back. These are telltale signs to proceed with caution. Some horses are sensitive enough that the moment you lay the pad on their back, you'll see them tighten their entire core. You may also see a concerned look in the eye and ears that turn backward.

Potentially even more dangerous are the horses that will act normally when you introduce the pad and place the saddle on for the first time. But, as you begin to tighten the girth, watch their eye. The first time you cinch it up, I go very cautiously, frequently petting

them and giving treats on occasion. Keep your feet slightly farther away from theirs than you usually think necessary. Some may jump quickly, and the last place you want to be pinned is too close or under a horse getting a saddle on for the first time.

Unfortunately, being cold-backed is a behavior that *cannot* be trained out of a horse. It *can* be made less severe and be dealt with (see p. 106). Many horses cope well if you can make the girth snug at first then take them for a short walk. This walk might be just out to the ring, where you can tighten the girth the remainder of holes. It's the shock of drastic increase of pressure that seems to set them off, so going slowly and steadily with a little walk in between seems to do the trick. Also I've found the more turnout you can give a cold-backed horse, the less the condition seems to appear.

by releasing the pressure and giving him a treat. Repeat a number of times so that the association is clear.

3 Now, apply light pressure to the bit alone where you're looking for the same response. If it does not happen, take a step back and repeat the simultaneous poll pressure.

Saddle

Similar progressive steps are used to introduce the saddle. Use your oldest saddle or the one in the worst condition for this task. It's unlikely, but should the horse happen to panic, you don't want to risk your best tack. I would also make sure that you have an appropriate-length girth to accompany the saddle. At this moment, you don't want to be in the position where you can hardly make the girth fit, struggling to get it on the last hole.

CAUTION: If your horse shows any nervous or anxious behavior, extra care should be used while tacking up (and mounting). Remember, there is no rush with horses—there's always another day. There is no reason that you have to do all you set out to accomplish at the start of the day. When the day is complete and you've taken even a small step forward, it's been a success.

1 First, put on the saddle pad. Slowly bring the pad near the horse, letting him sniff it if he likes, and place it on his back. Reassure him throughout the process that the pad is not going to attack him!

2 Once your horse is comfortable with the pad being taken on and off, it's time to introduce the saddle and the girth in a similar vein. Slowly place the saddle on your horse's back and gently attach the girth. Make sure to keep it quite loose initially and slowly tighten it. Tightening too quickly may startle him. Slow and steady will win the race! Keep in mind that some horses are what are known as "cold backed." Such a horse will panic when the girth is tightened too quickly. He might also stand like a statue while you tack him up and tighten the girth but the moment you walk forward, he feels the girth's restriction and, before you know it, he's galloping away bucking like a rodeo star (see sidebar on p. 31).

3 When you successfully have the saddle on your horse, take him for a walk so he has the opportunity to get used to the feel of it while moving around *without* the added complexity of being longed. All of the commands used before when working him in hand should still hold true with tack on.

Be very careful with how quickly you tighten and how tight you make the girth within the first few weeks. A girth tightening around their abdomen is a sensation that is not at all natural to your horse. If in doubt keep the girth on the loose side in the beginning.

A Learning Experience

One of the best horses I've ever ridden, Royal Tribute, can be just about as cold-backed as they come. He arrived as an enormous 17.3-hand, leggy, three-year-old gelding. In the process of starting him, our first clue that he might be cold-backed came Day Two of introducing the saddle. While he was standing on the cross-ties, I slowly secured the girth and he flinched just a moment. I had seen this before so I proceeded with caution: I unclipped the cross-ties and began to lead him forward.

One step was all it took for a tremendous athletic bucking display in the aisle—not exactly the ideal environment! I was able to get him back under control with a few quick tugs on the lead rope. From that point forward, I was extremely careful. I wore my air vest for the first few weeks when on his back. Unfortunately, just when I began becoming more complacent, he produced that trick out of his back pocket again.

In all my time riding, I've only had two horses that could send me sailing with just one buck: One of them ended up jumping Grand Prix circuits, and the second was Tribute. Luckily, at all times I landed on the ground unhurt and, it might sound strange, extremely excited, too—it's just so seldom that you come across a horse with such power that it makes the hair on the back of your neck stand up in awe.

Tribute has since all but set those bucking days behind him, though I will say that after he has been on "vacation," I have flashbacks on my first few rides. I finally relax after our first canter circle when I know I'm in the clear. Tribute won the USEA Futurity, the five-year-old Young Event Horse Championships and, to date, he has well over 10 wins through Preliminary Level and a second place at the Bromont CCI* in Canada as a six-year-old.

Longeing

Longeing is a very important skill to learn—for both horse and rider. It is a valuable tool whereby you teach your horse nearly everything you are going to do under saddle but from the safety of the ground. An additional benefit is that when you're away in an unfamiliar environment, you can take the edge off or prepare a horse for the show ring. Longeing is much safer than riding when you have a fresh horse that needs to burn off some steam; by the time you're ready to mount, you know you'll have a safe and productive session.

Equipment

There are a few vital required pieces. For you, gloves are a must! As I said earlier, there is nothing worse than a line burning your hand as it's pulled through suddenly by an inattentive or belligerent horse.

As for your horse, I always use a bridle and either a saddle or a surcingle so that you can add side-reins later. I also use boots for protection—on all four legs. It's especially important when horses are learning because they are not very aware of their legs. We use simple fleece-lined, velcro-strapped boots. They seem to hold up well and are easy to take on and off, as well as wash.

Stay firm and fair, but when the horse's attention is diverted, send him forward. This is the key to longeing—and riding!

Location

Look for an area that can be closed off so if you lose control your horse can't run frantically onto a road or into other paddocks. An indoor arena is a good place, as is a round pen.

Exercise

Your main goal when longeing a green horse is to teach the horse to *go* and *stop*. It's going to take a bit of time, but don't be happy until your command is responded to instantly. Any request for an upward transition should be achieved nearly instantaneously. A downward transition might take a moment longer. I'm always looking to see that the horse begins to respond as soon as the word leaves your mouth, but keep in mind it might take a few strides to complete the transition. When you ask a horse, you'll see in his eye and ears that your command has registered. Pay close attention to these subtle clues: If you ask and the horse gives you no response whatsoever, you need to make the aid more clear by asking again in a more stern manner.

1 The horse should feel confident about being led and responding to voice commands. So, to begin, lead him in a small circle, progressively lengthening the line. To assist in driving him *forward,* place your body toward his hindquarters. As you send him forward into walk, speak clearly and confidently. Depending on how responsive your horse is, you might have use the whip to assist your voice. Start with walk-halt and halt-walk transitions, just as you've been doing while leading.

2 When slowing down or stopping, place your body more toward his head. If you are in a fenced area or an indoor you can make use of the wall to help teach him how to stop. Walk from the center straight toward one of the walls with your horse. The wall will soon block his path forward: As he gets close to it, ask him to halt and the wall will act like an "emergency brake."

3 Once a lesson is solidified, use it to teach the next one. From the walk-halt, move on to walk-trot and trot-walk transitions. Remember, longeing is laying the groundwork for the horse to be ridden, where it's vitally important that his "brakes" work very well! With practice, you should be able to go from a full trot to a motionless halt in three strides.

4 After the horse is longeing well at the halt, walk, and trot, move on to canter. Each horse is very different. Keep in mind that some will find cantering on a 20-meter circle very difficult, while others can continue cantering all day long. If yours happens to find it hard, initially be happy with just a half a circle of canter. The important thing to remember is that once he's cantering, it's not acceptable for him to break into the trot (and leave him uncorrected) even after a great canter circle or two. Not that you need to get after him, but just regain the canter, hold it for a short while, and then ask for the trot. Make sure that every canter-trot transition is a result of your aid, not his desire. Every transition has to be your decision. Be very mindful that horses just being started under saddle have never worked this hard before. You are better off working for a shorter period of time than longer. You must always finish with a positive learning experience.

5 Let's look further into the canter, initially the hardest gait for a young horse being longed on a circle. It's often at this gait that a problem develops first. Let's say that yesterday you were able to get two continuous canter circles, but today he's breaking to trot after one-and-a-half. The kiss of death would be for you to keep pushing for your goal of two continuous circles. Even if he completely understands what you are asking, and is genuinely trying, he might not be physically able to complete the two circles today.

For a number of reasons this is not all that uncommon—he may be tired or sore from the day before. It would therefore be better to ask for just one circle and then a trot. At least, in this case, it is your idea to trot rather than him breaking to it. Your command is able to be performed, and he'll come away knowing that he should, and can, listen to you. Your relationship will be stronger when you are sensitive to his position. He is just starting out in this new world, and not only is it mentally, but physically challenging, too. So always ask him for something he's capable of doing well. When he's doubtful about your requests and loses trust, you're in trouble!

6 By the time your horse is *thinking forward* and can walk, trot, canter and halt on the longe line going in both directions, you're ready to introduce the side-reins. I like to use the leather side-reins with the rubber donut. There is some give to the reins, but it is limited. By using side-reins, you're looking to teach your horse to yield to pressure, stretch confidently forward into the bit, and begin to travel in a more consistent, efficient manner.

I like to attach them just below the flap of the saddle and at a length that gives the horse's head freedom to stretch in front of the vertical (figs. 3.3 A–C). Clip them on in the arena where you've been longeing. The moment they are on, calmly ask your horse to trot forward, and be prepared to use the whip to reinforce your voice. Keep in mind the most important thing here is for your horse to move forward and learn that by lowering his head, the pressure will go away. You don't have to be a stickler about keeping to an exact 20-meter

3.3 A–C In A, notice the side-reins are still slightly slacked to allow Simon's nose to go out a bit more. He is able to be at, or slightly in front of, the vertical. In B I've asked Simon to move into a trot and he has thrown his head up, catching the side-reins. Photo C shows the moment just afterward: He has softened again and is actively moving forward.

circle initially. A larger diameter or slight oval will work well and can be used to reduce pressure.

Do your best to reduce pressure on his mouth and if he's trying to raise his head, allow him to move out in an unrestricted manner. This is where the oval or larger circle can come in handy. Especially when he is just becoming accustomed to the side-reins, the moment he begins to stiffen and raise his head, employ the side-reins, soften your hand, and follow him forward onto a larger circle or short straight line. This way the only pressure on his mouth is from the side-reins and the moment he brings his head lower, the pressure will be released. If you try to stick to the *smaller* circle, you'll need tension on the longe line, which adds to the horse's pressure, thus making his reward less clear. It's difficult to predict a horse's first reaction: If you've done your homework your horse should already understand that he can yield from pressure on the bit by lowering his head. However, being alone out on the circle is an entirely new experience. The moment he makes contact with the side-reins, a horse will usually do one of two things: First and easiest, he'll yield and continue to trot. Second, he'll resist: He might try to stop, or worse, stop and begin to back up—a potentially dangerous situation because it's possible he might trip and fall, either over himself or by running into an object behind him. So if he starts to slow down or attempts to stop, quickly and firmly ask him to trot on, and if he does not quickly respond to your voice, get behind him with the whip.

If he does end up going backward, try to bring his head toward you to turn him as soon as possible. Keep in mind as long as he's running backward, additional pressure applied by you is bound to increase the backing-up speed. Changing the dynamic by turning him helps him begin to think forward. Then you can apply pressure.

Throughout the next week or so, progressively tighten the side-reins until you get to the point where the horse's head is held vertical when he stretches to the bit. Your goal is to have the horse very active, propelling himself from behind, and stretching over his back. Now you can start to vary the circle size and its location. Your neighbors will soon be convinced you've lost your mind, when they look out their window and see you doing big circles, small circles, and running down the long side along with your horse. Within reason, you should be able to do just about any figure, at any size and at any gait. Keep your total longeing time below 20 minutes and try to make it equal between left and right so not to add undue stress to any part of his body, especially at his young age.

It may take a week or two to get to the point where you can confidently put the side-reins on from the moment you step in the ring. Again, remember you must not attach them unless you're confident your horse is *forward thinking*. When in doubt, spend a minute or two without side-reins. You want a horse that is eager to work when he gets to the ring. In order to prevent him from becoming sour, reserve a few days each week to pony him on the trails or even take him on a long walk down the road. Just make sure he's not leaving the barn thinking, "Ugggghhh, I have to go to that darn ring again!"

chapter four

Training Step by Step:
Ridden Work

Mounting

Now that you've got your horse longeing well, it's time to get on for the first time. If at all possible, have an assistant along with you for the next few steps.

Exercise

1 Let's set up the conditions for success. Before mounting for the first time, you should longe your horse for 15 to 20 minutes in side-reins so he is effectively "in the zone" and working well. Now find a tall mounting block and a bucket of grain or other treats.

    With your helper holding your horse with the bucket of grain, slowly get up on the mounting block and pet your horse on the near, then the far side. Most horses will be completely comfortable with this; however, a few horses will get anxious as you step

tip *I prefer to use a mounting block because it allows you to more easily drape yourself over the horse's body in a progressive manner. Some people are comfortable mounting from the stirrup, and there is no question that the task can be accomplished that way, but there are more options when using a block for mounting.*

above them. In this case, try to move very slowly but with great confidence. If he does move—jumps forward or sideways—try your best not to react. The more upset he becomes, the calmer you should become.

2 Continue petting him all over his body then slowly lie across his back (figs. 4.1 A–C). Each step along the way, have your assistant give your horse a small amount of grain or a treat. You are looking for a positive association with mounting. I would leave it here on the first day; each subsequent day you should be able to lean on him with more weight until you're completely supported by your

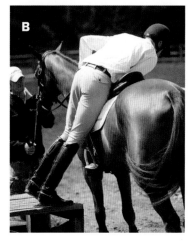

4.1 A–C With Conor's help at Simon's head, I am slowly beginning to apply weight to Simon's back in A. I am about half-supported by Simon in B. Note that I'm using my right elbow and forearm to try to add weight evenly across his back. I don't want to push him away from me. Simon is fully supporting me in C.

horse. Before mounting completely, you should be able to take the reins in your left hand and lie across the horse without him moving and without your helper needing to hold him. However, ask your assistant to stay close to your horse's head just in case something happens.

One trick that I've had great luck with is to have some treats on me—sugar always seems to work well. You can teach the horse that when you tap him on his far shoulder he should reach his head back for a treat. A common problem while mounting occurs when the horse's haunches step away so the beauty of this is that when he is expecting a treat, he'll wrap his head around to the right and his haunches just stay in place.

3 Finally, it's time to have your first ride! After lying over him for a few days, place your foot in the stirrup and lie across him; progressively adding a little more weight until you're fully supported in the stirrup and across his body. I am happy to have my body fully supported on and off a few times the first day, just standing still.

> The higher the energy level your horse is showing, the calmer you have to become to counterbalance his anxiety.

I like to use a halter and chain over the bridle with the lead rope in my hands—very much like an emergency brake. Your horse should have had the sensation of halter and chain for years at this point. The bridle and bit are still quite new to him, so if he starts to move faster than you are comfortable, simply use the reins and the lead, as well. You'll obtain the same nose pressure you had on the ground, as well as the pressure you exert on the bit. It's another way to break down exactly what is being asked by the rider from the horse. A rope halter will also work well here in lieu of the chain.

4 The next step is to walk forward. I've become more cautious over the years; I now find it easier to start the walking forward while still lying over the horse's back rather than sitting fully in the saddle. The great thing about this position is that if something bad happens, from a scoot, a noise, or a buck, you can very easily bail out and land on your feet. If you're sitting in the saddle, you're bound to have a much less comfortable landing.

To clarify, there are two ways you can lie across the horse. The first is just as you'd imagine: Lie over him like a dead man with your belly button just about in the center of the saddle. Keep in mind you'd like to keep just a small fraction more weight on the near side of the horse so that if you need to bail out, it's

4.2 A–E After lying across Simon's back, and confident that he is comfortable, I slowly proceed, eventually stepping fully into the stirrup, again with additional support on my right hand in an attempt to keep my weight distribution equal (A).

I use this position for the first few times I walk Simon forward (B). If something were to go wrong, it's very easy just to step down without risking injury, or possibly scaring him.

After I'm confident he is comfortable with me above him, with great care I will swing my leg over as slowly and gently as possible (C).

Notice my weight is again split between my left foot and right hand (D). It's incredibly important not to twist the saddle and torque Simon's back.

A lot of petting is in store for Simon at this point (E). I try to be as calm and relaxed as possible. Even if he tries to step forward, do your best not to react!

not onto your head. The second technique I often use when walking forward is to have my weight fully supported by my left foot in the stirrup and right hand on the far side of the saddle's knee roll. This way you're balanced across the horse but also have the ability to prevent going over the other side should some quick movement occur. Have your helper hang onto the lead line or the rein and lead you forward at the walk. I like to stop after 5 or 10 steps, each time saying "Whoa," or "Hooo," (whichever word you used during your ground-based work) when you ask the horse to stop; and say "Walk," when you ask him to go forward, with your helper rewarding him with treats throughout. Once this is uneventfully accomplished, I then pet him in front and behind the saddle, and slowly swing my leg over to sit completely in the saddle (figs. 4.2 A–E).

5 Your goal when teaching the horse the physical aids for going forward and steering is to put him in a situation whereby his "answer" to your request is the most obvious, logical one to him—and the correct answer (4.3. A & B). By this time, your horse fully understands your voice commands, so now you need to use them in concert with your physical aids. This way, the transition to use of physical aids is seamless and logical to the horse.

4.3 A & B
We are off on our own. The lead rope is still in my left hand so it can act as an emergency brake, if needed.

6 As you progress you can help your horse learn by having your helper longe you. You are the "voice" and "leg" asking for walk, trot or canter, but your helper is holding the longe line and whip to back up your requests, when needed. Keep this longeing up until you are completely confident that your horse understands the use of voice, leg and hand, and can be ridden softly at the walk and trot.

7 The next step is to start to refine your steering. When looking to turn, make full use of the opening rein. A horse will always be drawn to the place of least restriction. To turn right, for example, open your right rein at least 6 inches at the same time as you close your left rein and left leg. Training specific movements is beyond the scope of this book, but regardless of your eventual discipline, make sure to employ the same progressive building up and confirmation of aids. You will then produce a calm, confident partner for life.

Now that we have a horse that's successfully being ridden in the ring and out on the trials, let's recap what building blocks need to be laid to produce a confident and successful future for you and your horse.

Summary: Building Blocks

Quiet Confidence

From the very beginning, it's vitally important to remain calm and deliberate around horses because they are very intuitive and will, without fail, pick up on your personality. If you're a high-strung and nervous type, they will be too! People today are under a lot of stress—be it from work or at home—so make sure when you walk into the barn all of that baggage is left at the door.

Along with a relaxed overtone, be the confident human in charge. He will follow a strong person through fire and you are his leader! If you are lucky enough to live near a successful horseman, meet up with him, watch him move about the barn, and ride his horses. If you don't have this opportunity, watch as many interviews with such people; or, if you can get your hands on videos—especially of them warming up their horses—you'll learn an extraordinary amount. The very best are generally very grounded people. They have a quiet confidence that is intoxicating, and this personality trait is passed on to their horses. The best horses in the world might often seem a bit quirky, but they are *confident*, even cocky. They want to show what they are about and nothing will get in their way.

4.4 A-H Solid training is all about building blocks. Start small and progressively build on your successes. This sequence shows Darby jumping her very first cross-country jump. I've chosen a very small log with a clear approach and exit, but you can see that she has just about stopped and fallen to the right (A–C). I'm sitting back with a lot of leg and using a light tap with my crop in the right hand (D). As she jumps I'm behind the motion in order to press her across the log. At the same time, I'm allowing as much freedom as I can manage with my hand in an effort not to catch her in the mouth (E–G). Upon landing, I'm gathering my reins and getting back to a neutral balanced position (H).

Go Forward!

From the first interaction, your job is to instill in your horse that he always has a way to relieve the pressure you are applying, and that is to go *forward*—without fail. All too often when people become nervous around their horse, they become passive, unassertive, or even worse, a protectionist. Don't avoid potential confrontation: When your horse is scared of one end of the ring, or of a particular jump, become one with him. Be confident and assertive, and prove to him that nothing is going to "get" him!

Light and Responsive

Riding is an art when it is performed well. Make sure you have the most responsive and "light" partner possible in order for you to create a fine, finished performance. There is nothing more important than your horse being in front of your leg. Remember, you ask once lightly, and if this doesn't work, you *have* to get through to him. When you add your leg and "no one is home," then use a flick of your whip. Make sure you get a response. Without an attentive horse, you're sunk.

Logical Training Progression

Horses can only learn new things by associating them to something they already know—and know well—just as you started by leading before longeing, and longeing before riding. You need a systematic progression to produce a great horse. You have to walk before you run.

Remember, all of this takes time, and as I've said before, with horses there is no rush. They have their way of regulating this: When you're going too fast, they will let you know. Unfortunately, it usually shows up as some sort of behavioral or training issue, and the fix will *always* take much, much longer than the time that would have been spent to get it right the first time. Even dressage horses competing at the Olympic Games will constantly work to perfect the basic building blocks and when they are established, their exciting upper-level movements are no trouble at all. If there is no solid foundation behind them, they will lack brilliance—that is, if they happen at all.

chapter five

Behavior Problems:
A General Assessment

All horse-behavior problems, basic or complex, occur either from some sort of physical issue that is causing discomfort, or as a result of a step skipped in a horse's education.

Physical Issues

I'll discuss the physical cause first. It is critical, from the beginning, not to discount any medical issues that may be contributing to a horse's bad behavior. I've had countless horses come into the barn with a laundry list of problems, and the very first step is to assess whether or not there is a medical cause. One clear example is when a horse will only pick up his right lead and not the left. Often times this is a result of pain in his right hind and not him just being "difficult" or obstinate.

Maybe a horse is getting a little older and would benefit from some sort of joint maintenance. So if you suspect his behavior could be the result of pain, it's not a bad idea at all for a veterinarian to come out and do a quick exam. It's a very easy, inexpensive way to rule out any significant problems.

That said, however, I want to strongly caution you to be very careful not to make all problems you might have with a horse the result of a "medical issue." With horses you have to be very honest with yourself, and identify the abilities and limitations of both yourself and your horse. All too often over the years I've come across riders who attribute every behavioral problem their horse exhibits to a medical issue from the past.

This is all garbage! Horses are athletes and in the act of riding them, we're putting them under stresses that would not have been seen in the wild. Think about what it's like for you: When you're getting back into shape and you wake up in the morning with a little ache or pain, you are not stopped from performing at your peak. It won't stop your horse either! I once heard a great saying from the longtime coach of the USET, Jack Le Goff. The question was posed to him, "Do you think my horse has a problem that is preventing his progress?" Jack replied, "Yes, of course, it's the 'abscess' on his back!" It might seem over-the-top to liken *you* to an abscess, but any problem your horse has is almost always a problem of yours!

On the same theme, while your goal is to perfect your horse's performance as an athlete, you must hold yourself to this same standard. You will never be a truly effective rider if you are not in good physical shape. Personally, even though I ride 12 or more horses a day, I don't find this enough to keep me in peak condition. I try to ride a bike or do a workout with core-strengthening exercises six days a week. Consequently, my reactions are quicker and I can be more discrete with my aids, I am also less likely to inadvertently ask my horse for something due to a lack of control of my body.

Should a horse happen to trip and start to fall, a rider with good core strength and reactions can lean back quickly, which improves the chances of the horse being able to recover. A weaker rider will slump forward, landing on the horse's neck, which drives the horse into the ground. While this might be an extreme example, the same holds true for a downward transition. Watch Olympic-level dressage riders. Their position will be impeccable, and they remain the "rock" their horse can rely on. Be like those riders!

Educational Issues

When you have a horse that you had no part in starting, how do you know which training steps might have been missed in the past? Whether trying out a new horse, or dealing with your own horse showing some undesirable habits, first try to assess his state of training.

Below, I first give you the basic framework I use when riding a horse (brought to me with behavior issues) for the first time and when planning his training needs, and later, I'll address how you can find out what your longtime partner may have missed out on his training (p. 54).

Riding a New Horse

Getting the Lowdown

I make sure to speak in depth with an owner about a horse's history before getting on. I usually start with a few basic questions.

• *How old is the horse?* This gives you an insight into his life experience. Not that it's a fail-safe presumption, but the older horse will generally be less reactive and unpredictable. Younger horses, just like kids, will sometimes be silly and "spooky." Older horses are more domesticated, removed from their natural tendency to flee (or sometimes, fight). Knowing his age also gives me an idea of his physical well-being. If he is 18, I'm going to expect him to be a bit stiff and slow in his responses, initially. Some of his problem issues might be less due to a "bratty" personality and more a genuine reluctance.

• *What has he done?* What I mean by this is has he competed? What level of training is he confident performing? When I'm getting on a Fourth Level dressage horse, my expectations are drastically different than when mounting a First Level horse. That Fourth Level horse will be much more attentive, accurate and quick with his responses, and of course, I can ask a lot more of him.

Does he have any quirks? This is the most important question. My safety is paramount; yours should be too! Whatever the horse's problem, it's not worth getting hurt over. I had a mare brought over just the other day, and when I asked this question, her owner told me, "When you get on, she likes to rear and spin." So, of course, I was a bit more cautious while mounting. I tacked her up with my most comfortable, secure saddle. I got up in the middle of the ring—if I'm going to fall off, I'd much rather it be onto good footing: Picking driveway stones out of your elbow isn't all it's cracked up to be!

Get a heads up about what might be coming your way. Expect the best, but prepare for the worst, and minimize the risk to you—and the horse. With a truly tricky case, I'm not at all opposed to wearing a safety or air vest.

tip
When you take a horse to a professional for an assessment or training, be as forthcoming about his habits as you can. Even if your horse doesn't normally exhibit odd behavior, if there is a possibility, let the pro know. No one needs to get hurt—give a heads up!

Assessing Flatwork

Once you do actually get on the horse, you are ready to start a basic assessment.

- I like to start at the walk. Gradually, pick up the reins and take a contact. This will tell you right away whether this is a sensitive horse or a "bull." It also gives you a very good feel for whether he is naturally balanced or not. Within the first 30 seconds, you should be able to tell, with good certainty, whether he's naturally balanced or on the forehand, and on which side he's stiffer. You can determine how responsive he is to seat, leg and hand, and whether he's a natural born athlete or just a couch potato. Most importantly, in these first few moments, you should be able to tell what type of attitude he has: Is he benevolent, out to get you, or somewhere in the middle?

- The bull of a horse will be quite heavy while the sensitive one will be light to a fault in his contact. Most horses start off a bit lazily—not walking forward with conviction. Make the most of this initial opportunity to assess how responsive he is to your leg aids. I ask him to move on to a more forward, active walk. Right away, there'll be one of two possible answers: Either, he'll be responsive and move on appropriately (wonderful), or you'll find that when you apply more leg, he's indifferent or even moves less forward. Although, this latter response is obviously not ideal, at least I'm finding out right away that there is a flaw with the horse's training—he is not *thinking* about moving freely forward. This restriction has to be dealt with as soon as possible, because it will propagate throughout his training and make progress impossible.

• So I go to a few walk-halt and halt-walk transitions. As I ask him to walk, I'm going to use my whip lightly. If the response I am looking for doesn't happen, I repeat and use the whip with more conviction. However, you may be unfamiliar with the horse so you should exercise some caution about how hard you use the whip. I usually ask the owner how the horse responds to the whip: Some lazy horses will explode when touched with the whip, and I don't want to be caught off guard if that's going to happen. When no information is available, I get harder and harder with the whip but do it progressively. On a scale of one to ten, I start with a two or three before going to a six or seven.

A rider shouldn't have to nag her horse every step to continue walking. A horse needs to have a sort of "cruise control" installed. You should be able to ask your horse to move on at a certain speed, balance, tempo, and direction, and he should maintain it until you say otherwise. Many will quickly slow down or fall on the forehand. This is *not* acceptable. Lightly ask him back to your initial conditions; if it's ignored, quickly and firmly correct him. At this point, you've established that the gas and brakes work well!

It's paramount that you never start a "battle" you can't win!

• Now I'm going to check to make sure that I have steering. I'm going to start with just turning left and right—simple circles or other figures very quickly give you an idea of which of his sides is the stiffer one. Just like people, horses are stronger going on one diagonal over another. Your goal is to try and make him as ambidextrous as possible, while understanding he is going to have a naturally stronger side for life.

This is your first look into the horse's training, and it will foreshadow what may lie ahead. I do not ask the horse to back up in the first few minutes unless I know I have competent people on the ground. Basically, when you have a person on the ground, she can quickly come to the rescue and place her hands on the horse's chest (just as you did on the ground—see p. 28) to help explain what you're looking for. Without one, I wait to make sure I have all of the other components in place. Before you begin, you must have all the tools in case you open Pandora's Box!

• From the walk, move on to the trot. The same expectation of a prompt response is true for the transition to the trot. When you ask for the trot, the horse had better trot off with conviction.

• Once trotting with confidence in a forward active gait, move on to see what other "buttons" have been installed. If this is a horse with lateral tools in place, see how good they are. Start with a leg-yield, then on to shoulder-in, haunches-in, then half-pass, and lengthening and shortening.

• Then on to the canter. Much of the same strategies should be in place as found in the trot. Ask for the canter. It might start off well balanced, active and forward. Continue on and work to refine the horse's skill set.

Throughout all this work, you should have enough energy and the horse should be balanced and straight enough to maintain a steady, consistent contact. He should be rock steady with little input from the rider. There is no excuse for an "inelastic" connection at this point; holding his head down is nothing more than a "patch" that will not last.

Now that you've got a basic handle on the horse's flatwork you can begin to concentrate on improving the weaker aspects of it. And, if he is a jumping horse, let's see what he's made of and jump something!

Assessing Jumping

• For a horse that jumps, I like to start with a rail on the ground, usually trotted and cantered over on a circle. I like to use circles because it's very easy to identify when things start to go wrong. If your horse starts to overbend and drift, you'll be on a 25-meter circle instead of the 20 meters you started with. This will be clearly identifiable when riding and relatively easy to spot. You'll also have built-in safety: If he takes off or scoots, you can always spiral in until you regain control.

- His first time over the rail will tell you a lot. I like to be able to canter down and over the rail with neither the rhythm nor tempo changing. (*Rhythm* is defined as the sequence of footfalls in each gait, whereas the *tempo* is the frequency of those footfalls.) If the horse quickens his tempo on the approach, reduce the size of the circle until you're able to keep the tempo constant.

- Assuming you can canter the ground pole without issue, move on to a small jump. Depending on the horse's history, you may progress quickly to much bigger fences, while a greener horse might stay quite small for some time. I would progress off the circle to longer approaches and introduce some bending lines and combinations.

- Another critical skill that you need to assess is the horse's *adjustability*. A very easy test is to set up a 60-foot line of two verticals. See if you can ride the distance between them in four, five, then six or more strides, being very particular that your horse remains straight as an arrow before, during, and after the exercise. Obviously, with each stride added between the jumps the horse has to shorten his step. Allowing him to "wiggle" is not productive because he is just giving himself more distance by doing this so he doesn't have to shorten his step. Once you have confirmed that you can both add and subtract strides when you want, you should have an accurate assessment of the horse's strengths and weaknesses.

tip *When jumping on a circle, always be sure you're jumping on an exact circle. If the "circle" becomes an oval, you'll have considerably less success when attempting to get a straight approach on takeoff. Moreover, a circle also allows you to maintain the bend throughout, and it tends to produce a horse with a softer, rounder topline—and subsequently a better bascule over the fence. Once you're able to maintain his balance and keep the tempo consistent, begin to bring that circle out to an oval where you can begin to introduce a straight-line approach. If something goes awry just return to the circle until it's sorted.*

Evaluating Your Own Horse

Let's add to what we discussed about evaluating a *new* horse and examine what might have been missed in your current horse's education (that is, the horse you have *now*). Here's how to identify "skipped steps" in your horse's foundation.

As I briefly covered in the previous section, you need to get a baseline on your horse. It is often helpful to have a professional come and give you a second, unbiased opinion. All too often—and it even happens with the best riders in the world—you get "wrapped up" in the horse's history. It's very easy to say, "He used to run," or "He used to grab the bit," or "His last owners scared him," as three examples, then continue to ride defensively to prevent that fault. Once a problem has been resolved, the most difficult—but critical—skill you need as a rider is to be able put it behind you. Keep an eye out for it, but don't ride as if it's always there. Your horse *can* and *will* change over time. You must expect your horse to step up to the next level.

Flaws in your horse's foundation will be clear from the beginning: Problems that exist in the walk will generally show up in the trot and canter. These need to be ironed out so progress can be made. What are some quick easy tools to help you diagnose your horse?

Creating a Brave Partner

It's within your power to create a brave partner. Once you're able to jump around a small course and have moderate control of your horse's balance with his tempo remaining consistent, it's the perfect time to introduce some "scary-looking" fences. Keep in mind, when you point your horse at a jump, his job is to jump it. Regardless of line, distance, approach, color—he has to jump!

Intimidating jumps can use a tarp or horse cooler draped over the top rail; be made of fake rocks; be in obnoxious colors; or be very narrow. Be creative! The most important thing is that they are small enough to be jumped from a standstill—that is, roughly one foot tall. Keeping them small will allow you the best opportunity to jump them without fear of overfacing your horse. Even the most careful horses will not lose confidence because they forget a hind leg: At a foot tall, the consequences of a mistake are minimal. However, mentally, this can prove a sufficient challenge for your horse.

Transitions
Your horse will either be attentive and prompt, or he won't. When he isn't responsive enough, progress will be limited.

Steering
By this I don't mean can you turn left or right, but can you move individual parts of your horse's body independently? Turns-on-the-haunches and forehand should be elementary. Can he spiral in and out? Can he leg-yield and perform a shoulder-in or half-pass? Can you string them together without issue? While some of these are advanced maneuvers, you should start to lay the groundwork from Day One.

Brakes

Can you stop on a dime? If not, you have a problem! Not only should it be of concern that he *can* stop quickly, but it is vitally important *how* he stops. Does he halt by doing a nosedive into the dirt or gently lowering his haunches into the halt while keeping an uphill balance? You should have the ability to start or stop at will. When the brakes are worn out or improperly installed, they must be fixed. Lots of transitions are in your future!

Ride the horse you have today, not the one you had yesterday.

Jumping

Can you jump a fence of small height without changing the line, pace, balance, or disturbing the rhythm? Can you turn before or after, or jump at an angle? Does he toss his head before or after the jump?

The most common skipped or misunderstood steps in a horse and rider's education are:

• *The horse's response to aids.* Many riders are not attentive enough to their horse's response to pressure. As I've been saying, when you add a light pressure you must get a prompt and active response. An inattentive horse has to be dealt with promptly or progress cannot be made.

• *The horse not going forward (the source of nearly all resistance).* This is tied in with yielding from the leg, but it's also the overall feel you get when watching or riding a horse. Is there a spring in his step? Or does it appear as if he's moving along in deep mud? Does he have natural power and cadence? He should, and it should be improving over time.

• *The rider's judicious use of aids.* Nag, nag, nag! Don't be a pest to your horse. It's very important that a rider pays close attention to her equitation and use of aids. Not just that you sit up with a straight line from your elbow to the bit but that you are not inadvertently giving aids or signals to your horse that you don't intend to give. When you use your leg properly, it should be hardly visible to someone on the ground. If you're kicking like an eight-year-old, you're bound to be just about as effective. Be discrete and quiet, and expect results. Walk softly but carry a big stick.

• *The use of a crop or whip.* I carry a crop or whip on nearly every horse I ride with very few exceptions. When used correctly there is no reason that your horse should care whether you carry one or not. As a rider, it's a critical tool that will allow you to produce a higher degree of precision from your riding and your horse's performance. Remember, just because you have it doesn't mean you have to use it, but when needed, it's important it is there for you.

• *The rider's voice.* Your voice should be used sparingly—it is incredibly helpful with younger and greener horses, but as horses gain experience, I use my voice less frequently with a few exceptions.

I do still use "Ho" or "Whoa" with horses of all ages, when jumping. It, too, must be trained, but when used effectively, it can give a horse advanced warning that he is getting too deep to a fence. It is also another way a rider can ask for rebalancing without "physically" disturbing the horse's balance when jumping.

I'm not a big advocate of clucking, in that most people don't use it correctly. Ninety-nine percent of the time, when I ask a rider to stand her horse in the middle of the ring on a loose rein and cluck, I hardly see the horse twitch an ear. If you're going to cluck, you have to train it like your leg: Cluck and instantly use your whip to reinforce the message. It could be a valuable tool; if you're going to use it make sure, like the whip, that it's seldom used, but always noted by your horse.

PART 2
Let the Games Begin

Before You Begin:
Horse and Rider
"Self Examination"

Riding is a game, and regardless of how forgiving your horse is, he will be constantly exposing weaknesses in your foundation and training system. Problems you see in your horse are a reflection of *your* training. Stay objective and slightly removed from the situation; any emotional response will be counterproductive. Think of all of these so called "problems" as challenges alone. Finding the solution to the puzzle presented by your horse can be addictive!

I'm now going to briefly review some of the information I presented in Part One where I discussed how you should evaluate a horse with behavioral issues and your own riding ability. I'm repeating it because I feel that before you embark on dealing with any horse problem (beginning on p. 65), you need to take an honest look at your horse and at your own current skill set.

Evaluating the Horse

Ask Yourself:

• *Is your horse's "problem" physical?* As I mentioned, I strongly recommend having your trusted veterinarian out to the farm for a basic soundness exam to rule out any physical issues or to give you a better idea of treatments that could improve the horse's situation. Upon the conclusion of this assessment, you can expect to have an idea from your vet of any limitations your horse might have. It might seem like common sense: There is no reason to ask a horse to do something he is not physically able to perform. After you've ruled out any medical diagnosis, you can move on to the problem at hand and look to correct it.

• *Does your horse's behavior issue have its roots in a missing component of his training foundation, or does it stem from "attitude"?* First, maybe there was some sort of building block skipped or rushed (a *foundation flaw*) that caused the horse not to completely understanding what is being asked. Think of this like a person who doesn't entirely comprehend a language—it just happens to be the language of the equestrian sports.

Second, when the horse has an "attitude," the behavior can have more "malicious" roots, since the horse fully understands what is being asked and is simply ignoring you, or worse yet, actively working against you. You might ask, aren't they related? Of course they are, but I think the real distinction is the horse's disposition. So, how do you determine if your horse is just ignorant or being belligerent?

Let's take the leg-yield as an example. (After you have the walk, trot, and canter down, this is the first lateral movement you teach the horse.) Here are two sample scenarios to help figure this out:

Sample Scenario One: Foundation Flaw

A horse that has a missing link in his training might react to the same aids in a similar fashion—he might not move laterally, or not at first, and get a bit heavy in your hand. And after you use an opening outside rein and close your fingers and add your inside leg he starts to "pop" his shoulder. But if you pay close attention, he didn't move into your leg pressure.

He didn't pin his ears or swish his tail while sucking back. His response wasn't exactly what you wanted, but it was in the right direction, and was done without exhibiting any aggressive, malicious behavior.

Sample Scenario Two: "Attitude" Problem
First turn down the quarterline, put your inside leg on, and a supporting outside rein. Let's say your horse does not move sideways at all; in fact, you notice the swishing of his tail, his ears going back, and as you increase your leg pressure, he seems to move *into* your leg rather than yield away from it. He may also start to "suck back" as leg pressure increases. This is a clear sign that he has primarily an attitude problem, which means you will have to become more assertive to get your point across and sway his opinion. In this case, your horse has clearly reacted to your aids, but in a disingenuous way. Some horses may start off down the same path as this example and still just be ignorant, but as soon your aids escalate and he appears to actively work against you, you have a horse that needs an attitude adjustment.

Evaluating the Rider

Ask Yourself:
• *Can you handle the horse's problem?*
I want to help you develop a concrete plan about which challenges you are able to attack alone; which ones you may need help with; and which might just be better left to a professional trainer. Regardless, the way to truly improve is to be completely open and honest with yourself: Only through a thoroughly objective assessment will you be able fix the issues that could limit your success. So to begin, do your riding ability and confidence level enable you to safely address your horse's issue?

• *Do you have a personal goal in mind?*
If not, one needs to be established. Where would you like to be with horses in two weeks, two months, or two years down the road? It is very important to set attainable goals; without them it's very easy to flounder about without improving.

• *Are you mentally prepared to improve?*
A change in your habits or expectations may be as intimidating as riding your bucking horse or worse! In order to improve you must set up realistic goals and go after them with conviction. Don't sell yourself short. You have the ability to improve so go out and get it!

• *Are you at the right barn?*
Sometimes barn dynamics can hinder your progression. I find a lot of people get stuck in their barn's hierarchy of rider ability. Keep an eye on your goals, and don't let anyone stop you. You *can* achieve more.

• *With your goal in mind and the environment ripe for improvement, is your horse truly able to reach that goal with you?*
When your answer is "Yes," this is ideal! Keeping your goal in mind and using the specific skills needed to succeed, get out to the barn and start working!

When your answer is "Maybe," it is probably because very often, like me, you will not be exactly sure how far a particular horse can go. As long as you enjoy riding him every day and you are progressing, keep working. And when progress slows to a crawl, try to figure out what's stopping it. If it's the horse's talent alone, and your goals are to achieve more, then it might be worth thinking about moving on to another horse.

When your answer is "No," it is definitely time to think about getting another horse. I'm the first to say that if you are happy where you are and just looking to ride him, great! However, even though frustrated with his limitations, many people are so attached to their horse, they give up trying to achieve their goal, and even get turned off riding, which is a great shame. There are plenty of people out there willing to give your horse a fabulous home and love him as much as you do. Allow him to move on, so you can achieve your goals with another horse.

• *Are you willing to make the best of the opportunity you have with your horse?*
When your answer is "Yes," get ready to work hard! Progress will come to those who work the hardest and smartest. It's not easy, but well worth it.

When your answer is "No," again, it might be time to look for a different partner. There are an unlimited number of horses available.

• *Do you know when it's time to go to a professional trainer for lessons?*
Limited resources, stubbornness, or a reluctance to be critiqued may make regular lessons difficult, but the benefits are well worth the cost! Ask a friend to come along with you and have her video the entire lesson. Two positive outcomes will result: First off, you'll relive the lesson an unlimited number of times. (I've got news for you: The bad habits you work on in your lesson will improve, but they will *not* go away after that hour!)

The second beautiful thing about having another "educated" eye watching your lesson is that she'll be able to see what the instructor is pointing out and remind you of it next time you are riding together. Stretch your training dollars out!

tip *I'm a huge fan of videoing my riding. Videos are the single best learning tool at your disposal, and the great thing is that they are virtually free, as long as you have friends! An instructor can tell you all day long that you have some bad habit that needs to be fixed, but it doesn't hit home until you see it for yourself.*

• *What do you need to improve before dealing with the horse's specific problem(s)?*
Every horse has some particular weaknesses that will limit his progress unless you can handle the issues. Perhaps you have dealt with a similar horse in the past with success? If not, do you have the skills to tackle the job? It's a good idea to figure out which of your skills need further refinement. Ask your instructor to whittle down your riding flaws to a "Top Five" list. At the same time, do a quick self-assessment and write down your own Top Five skills that need improvement. Combine these lists, and make it your mission to reduce this new list to zero!

• *Do you have the desire—and time—to dedicate to solving your horse's issues?*
For some horses to succeed, a significant amount of time is required. It can mean you'll need to ride them six or seven days a week.

• *Is fear limiting your potential?*
Both these last two questions must be answered before embarking on this journey. If either answer is not in the affirmative, maybe you should consider a different horse—one that knows the ropes a bit better so that you can enjoy your limited time in the saddle without seriously testing your confidence every time you get on.

Throughout this book, I'll be giving you specific tools to combat a large number of issues, but at the end of the day, you are the one on your horse's back, so you'll need to use your instinct, gut feeling—and talent—too.

The Common Problems Most Riders Can Solve

I've selected the problems most usually seen when training horses to cover in this book. Each issue is explained in a way to better understand what the horse is thinking, then how you can best resolve it!

On the pages ahead you'll find three sections devoted to three types of training problems: Section I covers Contact Issues (p. 65); Section II discusses Unruly Outbursts (p. 91); and Section III consists of Jumping Problems (p. 133).

Contact Issues

E veryone would love to have a steady soft contact with their horse's mouth, but, unfortunately, when riding, you are sometimes unable to keep your horse's head steady.

A horse is happiest when he is able to stay in harmony—he is looking for a quiet, reliable partner. But, for various reasons, a horse may have a nagging problem that makes remaining steady uncomfortable for him, so he moves his head to escape pressure. At their root, contact issues are an external sign of unrest.

Unsteady or inconsistent contact is a pervasive problem seen in all riding disciplines. Many people describe it as "not accepting the bit" or "not accepting the contact." I like to think of a horse's head and neck like the dashboard gauges in your car that give you information about the car's working parts and engine. When you see an unsteady head, it's actually letting you know that you don't truly have your horse engaged and working well from behind: A good solid contact should be a result of consistent thrust and balance originating from the horse's hindquarters. When riding, I like to have a constant, but *light* contact, which should be unwavering and even—from left to right. Keep the German Training Scale in mind: Rhythm, Suppleness, Contact, Impulsion, Straightness, and finally, Collection. In order to have a good contact, your horse must have a consistent rhythm and be relaxed and supple. The Scale is just a framework to keep in mind when training a horse.

First Rule Out: Physical Causes

▶ Cause One

Tooth discomfort is often the root of your horse's unrest. Without regular care, sharp edges can form that make the bit very uncomfortable.

Solution

Make sure your horse's teeth are in good shape. I have our dentist out every six months to ensure that our horses' mouths are in great overall condition.

▶ Cause Two

Severe, harsh, and sharp bits.

Solution

I've had a number of horses come into our barn with unsteady contact issues, and many are using Happy Mouth bits. These bits are great most of the time: They are forgiving and many sensitive horses are happier using them. However, I must caution you to keep a close eye on their condition. In recent years I've steered clear of using them: Since the metal mouthpiece is covered in plastic, once your horse begins to chew on it, the bit can suddenly become quite sharp—without any warning. You go from one of the most forgiving bits out there to one that is as painful as you can get.

This sharp edge is trouble enough to deal with at home, but when it occurs as you are walking over to the warm-up area at a show, it can be responsible for the end of your day. With a little bad luck, your horse might bite it just "right" and without you realizing, you'll enter the ring with a bloody mouth. This, of course, is grounds for elimination. It's not worth the risk, in my opinion.

There are many alternatives: You can wrap a normal metal bit with a soft latex compound that comes in a roll, like tape. The bit will never get sharp, and will be just as forgiving, if not more so, than a Happy Mouth. Aside from wrapping, leather and straight rubber or plastic bits are suitable, too. Keep in mind, wrapped bits might not be legal for some competitions. Check your rulebook or consult the technical delegate (TD) or steward when you arrive at a show or event to make sure what you're using is permitted.

It is also worth mentioning that using a severe bit often causes the horse pain that accounts for the inconsistent contact you are experiencing. When in doubt, it's best to swap your bit for a less harsh option.

A bit that uses leverage will often cause unsteadiness. These include some hackamore bridles, hackabits, and elevator bits. If you are riding with one, check to see if it's possible to reduce the leverage. Many times this will fix the problem.

▶ Cause Three
A small percentage of horses are hypersensitive to light.

Solution
Speak to your vet if the following description fits your horse: He works well 99 percent of the time, but when in direct sunlight, either passing the door in an indoor arena, or while riding outside, he sharply "twitches" his head. He may even pop the reins out of your hands. As soon as the twitch has started it stops again, and he goes back to work almost as if nothing ever happened.

A light-sensitive horse shows signs of this all year long. The easiest test is to ride in an indoor with windows. First, ride in the shady section and if the twitching doesn't occur there move on to the sunny parts (or go outside) where the sun-sensitive horse will begin to show signs of discomfort.

Many horses that react to the sun are much better off with sunblock on their nose. And there is a net that fits over the noseband and blocks the nostrils from light. Again, check the rules about using the netting before competition.

▶ Cause Four
Just like people, horses suffer from allergies. If you notice your horse's contact unsteadiness is concentrated during certain times of the year, this very well might be your cause.

Solution

Allergies are a whole different ballgame and more difficult to identify as a cause. There are allergy tests for horses, which I've used with some success. If you suspect your horse is reacting to some allergens, I highly recommend scheduling an appointment with your veterinarian for further investigation.

If your vet finds that your horse is susceptible to some allergens there are treatment options available, the easiest of which is avoiding a certain type of food or bedding, while the more complicated conditions can be treated with an allergy kit. Following blood testing, an allergy kit is produced that consists of a number of injection vials containing a mix of low and increasing doses of the particular allergens that affect your horse. They effectively desensitize his system. These daily injections are given subcutaneously, and it generally takes a few months to complete the series. They are very effective for skin irritants; slightly less so for respiratory conditions. You would hope that this sort of problem is mentioned when you are thinking about purchasing a horse since there is no "training" solution. Make sure to ask a seller if the horse has any special needs. Personally, I avoid purchasing a horse that has severe allergies.

Now that you've ruled out the physical causes that can interfere with a consistent contact, I'll discuss the familiar problems that occur and suggest some training solutions.

Contact Training Problems

Grabbing the Reins

What Happens

When the horse grabs the reins, yanks the bit, or flips his head, and he succeeds in lengthening the reins or displacing the rider, this behavior has been rewarded. He will then begin to pull the same trick again and again.

▶ Cause One

The first reason for this is simply ignorance—you see it in a baby or green horse that doesn't fully comprehend what you are looking for with contact. These horses may slowly shake their head or grab a rein and drag you around. Often they are difficult to steer and, in general, feel "dull."

Solution A

Exercise

1 You should have a light feel of the horse's mouth and ask him to move forward—regardless of gait—and the moment he grabs or locks on to a rein, immediately close your fingers on both reins to quickly increase the amount of pressure. At the same time as you increase this pressure on the rein, apply a significant amount of steady leg pressure primarily on the same side of the stiffness. This is not a kick, but rather a sharp squeeze.

2 The horse will probably resist for a moment, but you should not be deterred—just keep pressing on. The amount of leg and hand pressure should gradually increase until the point where the horse yields. This should happen quickly, but if it doesn't, start increasing the bend to the inside until he yields. Once he does, you must quickly release the pressure without completely dropping the contact; your goal is to not have a loop in the rein. Be as light as possible, retaining a line of communication with your horse

3 In the "reward" phase you must soften the contact to just under a pound, but enough to maintain contact with the bit (*without* looping the rein). A horse will be reluctant to seek the contact if he is unconvinced it will be there every time. The other concern here is that if you've had to increase the bend to the point where the horse "unlocks," you should immediately allow him to straighten out. He will not be able to sustain any sort of pushing power when he is not straight and confident in the *outside* rein. The key to riding well is that once the horse gives, you must quickly reward him. Repeat this process every time he even starts to think of grabbing onto the rein.

For example, your ideal contact could be a pound or so, but when he grabs the rein, that might increase all the way to 10 or more pounds. However, the moment he yields, it immediately goes back to the "pound-or-so" level. A common rider error is to over-reward by completely dropping the contact; this tends to produce a horse that is unsteady, which doesn't exactly fix the issue!

4 What separates amateur riders from professionals? Professional riders are able to identify when they start to "lose" the horse and react while the problem is still small. Amateurs do not recognize it until the problem is further developed and subsequently larger and harder to fix. In order to improve your effectiveness, try to pick out the patterns presented by your horse: When you're able to pick up a clue four strides before the entire "lock up" has happened, you'll have a much better chance at stamping it out quickly.

Solution B

The second option to help pros and amateurs alike is to go back to longeing with side-reins (p. 34). Side-reins are very quick to reward the horse for a job well done. They work on the same principle as Solution A: The moment the horse starts to stiffen, the pressure increases and it will not be reduced until the horse yields. Soon enough, the horse learns to yield to the smallest increase of pressure (fig. I.1).

I.1 When longeing is used to start horses, it can have tremendous benefits later in the horse's life. Remember, you can add a lot more complexity to longeing—it doesn't have to just be circle after circle. Be creative: Add transitions, changes in gait, change the size and shape of the circles, and even add ground poles. All of these will greatly help your horse!

▶ Cause Two

The second type of head-flipping or unsteady contact is a more malicious sort. This is where the horse intentionally grabs one rein—or both. It's very important in this case to determine exactly the cause of the disobedience. Horses are creatures of habit, and most behavioral problems start to show a consistent trend: They can be set off by a particular object, occurrence or situation. It could be a jump that they've decided they don't like, a dog, or simply another horse in the ring. It could also be related to leaving the in-gate, or wanting to return to the crowd in the warm-up area. In all cases, this habit must be dealt with promptly.

Solution A

In these cases, you must be more aggressive in your correction. The difficult part of this behavior lies in its unpredictability. Many times it more likely happens in one location or circumstance, but this isn't a 100-percent-reliable predictor. Your riding position is very important for you to be effective and ready to tackle whatever your horse throws at you.

When a rein (or reins) is grabbed, you should not loosen your grip or get pulled forward. You see this happening all the time with kids on a pony that wants to eat grass: He drops his head and the kid is instantly lying on his neck. The same holds true for adults. Their horse might not be eating grass, but when their reins are yanked their upper body is pulled forward. Riders are then forced to release the contact, letting the reins become longer, and voilà, the horse has won!

So it's absolutely critical that your lower leg is in a secure-enough position and your upper body is tall so that when force is applied to the reins it actually anchors you deeper in the saddle (see figs. III.15 A–E, p. 159).

Solution B

If you're unable to stay secure in the saddle, you have a few options. Some people might advocate using a stronger bit, but I would be hesitant. When the horse does soften, you want to be able to reward him with a forgiving contact and if the bit is too harsh, it is impossible keep that soft "feel."

CAUTION: It's very important with all of these training problems not to allow your horse to finish the day with the upper hand. If it means that you ride first and have to finish up with longeing, so be it.

Solution C

Go back to longeing before each ride and make sure not to use the full elastic side-reins. Use the leather ones with the rubber donut, or you can use just the straight leather side-reins without. You want the stronger, less flexible option so there is a consequence every time he grabs the bit. You could also look for a local professional who can get on your horse and not be pulled into the same trap (see Tip, p. 73).

Head-Tilting

What Happens

The horse has an imbalance in his body and relies on one rein only in order to compensate. This causes his head to tilt to one side.

Head-tilting is a problem generally encountered when you are working on the flat. In competition, each movement in which the horse is tilting his head will be marked down. It is an indication of a lateral imbalance.

▶ Cause One

Let's take an example where the horse holds his nose to the right and his poll to the left—the contact on the left rein is stronger. There is an imbalance leading to this head tilt, which can be a weakness in the horse, or more likely, just a training issue.

Solution

When riding, you're going to need to get this horse off, or "lift," his left shoulder. Exercises to help with this are: leg-yielding left or shoulder-in right. (Note: You should carry your left hand slightly higher than the right, keeping the bit in the corner of his mouth to help straighten him.) The important thing is not to just take a consistently stronger hold of the left rein, because you will become the "crutch" without which he cannot balance, thus making the problem worse. Work with both leg-yielding and shoulder-in interspersed with short lengthening exercises.

tip *When you send a horse out to a pro, it is best to send him for at least two weeks so the habit can be properly dealt with. After your horse is there, I strongly recommend going to visit on a regular basis so that you can be taught the methods that are working best. Consistency is key when training horses. You'll get the most for your money when you can observe the professional narrating his ride and describing what he is doing to fix the problem as it occurs. I would also have him ride your horse first, and when he thinks it is appropriate, have you get on to feel what he's been working toward.*

A trainer can describe to you all day long what something should feel like when it's performed correctly, but until you feel it first hand, you won't fully comprehend it.

For the horse to truly soften, he needs to become further engaged, so lateral work supplemented by exercises that will activate the hindquarters will give you great results. Stair-step a leg-yield across the diagonal or ride a few steps sideways alternated with a few steps of lengthening. The lengthening will get the hind leg farther underneath the horse's body and the lateral movement will help him become more engaged and subsequently lighter in your hand.

▶ Cause Two

Rider balance and equitation play a significant role in the performance of the horse. Oftentimes a rider will collapse on one side of her body and so influence the horse in a crooked fashion. In the situation that I discussed above where a horse tilts his nose to the right, the rider may very well be collapsing her rib cage on the right, which will lift her *right* seat bone and render it ineffective. The rider's weight at this point is pressing the horse down onto his *left* shoulder.

Solution

I can't overstate how much an assistant can help from the ground. I would search out the most qualified person with an educated eye for dressage that you can find in the area. If no one is available, a video camera is your best friend. It does not lie, and you have the opportunity to slow the video down and replay it to explore all your weaknesses. When recording, it is most helpful to have the friend with the camera stand in the center of a circle while you ride around her. This way, you'll have a consistent viewing angle and distance; changes are more clear from a grounded vantage point.

Grinding Teeth

What Happens

Teeth grinding is where your horse grinds his lower jaw repeatedly, causing an audible noise. Horses often grind their teeth from anxiety or when they are nervous because they do not understand what you want. This can be one of the most frustrating behaviors because when a judge hears the horse grinding his teeth in the ring, you will be penalized. Most often the habit's origin stems from the horse's initial training.

▶ Cause One

Most often associated with nervousness when the horse doesn't understand what is being asked, the behavior is similar to the child who twirls her hair.

Solution A

When you present a new concept your horse may begin to grind. This is a very clear demonstration that he is not yet ready to take that next step. I would go back a few notches and revisit concepts that are clear. It will make him feel like a rock star! Then, touch on the new exercises again in a few days. If you don't hear the grinding, you can proceed with caution.

Solution B

If you are simply doing exercises with your horse that you are sure are confirmed and he is grinding his teeth, there are other options. Some horses respond well to a very quick tug at the reins so the moment the grinding starts, give a very quick, sharp tug. If the grinding stops immediately following the tug—even for a moment—you have a shot at training the behavior out of him.

So, the moment you hear the grinding, give a quick tug on the reins. Repeat this process indefinitely. You'll increase your odds of success if you also back off and reduce the complexity of what you are asking.

▶ Cause Two

If you are given, or have bought, a horse that is further along in his training and he is grinding his teeth, then you have a bigger task at hand. This is obviously an established habit that may never disappear. Slowing your training progression can help, but you have to be aware that he may continue to grind his teeth regardless. So I like to think of this as switching to "damage control."

Solution
Made specifically for the show ring, there are treats produced for horses that grind their teeth. They are wax and sugar tabs, and when fed they usually eliminate the sound the teeth make—at least, for the short term. I've heard of hundreds of other "remedies," anything from peanut butter, to grain, to sand, some of which just sound downright cruel. The other thing you have on your side is that most judges are "in the zone," so to speak, so often do not notice the sound.

▶ **Cause Three**
Occasionally, you will find a very smart horse that is bored—and consequently, anxious—doing basic exercises. This horse's mind is running at full speed, so give him something else to focus on.

Solution
Begin to introduce more complicated figures or more frequent transitions. Also, keep in mind that a rubber bit may very well make the problem worse in that it "invites" the horse to chew or gnaw on it. Substitute the rubber with a thick metal bit; it will be forgiving enough, without the unwanted side-effect.

Tongue Issues

What Happens
Your horse sticks his tongue out, either to the side or straight ahead. Tongue issues are usually deep-rooted in a horse's past, and are generally a method by which the horse can avoid full acceptance of the bit.

Tongue issues are even more frustrating to deal with than the grinding. While some judges' hearing may not be spectacular, their vision is usually quite good. Every time they see a tongue, your score plunges! A small caveat here is that if the tongue is coming directly out of the front of the mouth it should not be scored down.

▶ Cause Three

This problem is most prevalent with horses off the track or poorly started, but in nearly all cases it has to do with their not properly accepting the contact. They usually stick their tongue out on one side and lock on to that rein.

Solution A

Somewhat like the head-tilting (see p. 72), you should try to get your horse lighter and lighter in your contact. In most cases a horse sticks his tongue out at the same time he attempts to lean or lock on to the rein. For this example, let's say the horse's tongue sticks out of the left side of his mouth.

Leg-Yielding

When a horse is learning the leg-yield, I initially allow his shoulder to pop slightly while pushing him off my inside leg, in that he is, at least, moving laterally. I then ask for a bit more bend and add more inside leg. What you'll notice is that you can get the idea across quite quickly by increasing the bend until the haunches move laterally. As soon as they do, decrease the bend and ask as you would with a more educated horse. Soon after, he might pop the shoulder again, but again increase the bend and apply more inside leg. As he starts to catch on, you can increase the frequency and decrease the amount of bending, seeing that he'll respond more quickly. Soon enough, you'll be able to keep just a very slight flexion to the inside, and he'll move over laterally without a problem.

Exercise

1 Start with leg-yielding away from the side the tongue sticks out (if the tongue is out on the left, push him off the left to the right), from the quarterline to the wall as well as from the wall to the quarterline. Keep in mind that in a correct leg-yield you have a slight flexion at the poll around your inside leg and *away* from the direction of travel. The goal is to get him moving off your yielding (inside) leg and stepping into the opposite rein enough so you are able to momentarily drop the contact on the inside without losing the bend.

2 From leg-yielding, move on to shoulder-in. In the end, you're looking to create the same light feel you were able to create with the leg-yield but with more engagement and subsequent pushing power, without the tongue appearing. The moment you see it, you have to take a step back to get him lighter again on the side the tongue appeared. When he's better balanced and supple again, the tongue should recede. Your job is to identify his weak side. Use exercises to strengthen him so that he is equally light on both reins. This horse with his tongue hanging out on the left should, in most cases, always be cured by pushing him off or away from the left leg while trying to get him to take a more solid connection on the right rein.

Solution B

Like teeth grinding (see p. 74), some horses respond to a quick tug on that rein. It really depends how entrenched the habit is in your particular horse. When he takes his tongue in just after the tug on the rein, you're in good shape. Simply repeat the process, and over time, the behavior should at least be reduced, if not eliminated altogether.

tip *A horse with tongue issues usually does better with a lighter contact. I always try to ride him in a way so I can keep a feather-light feel. The moment I start to lean on him, the tongue usually comes out.*

Solution C

When it comes to a competition, you need to have tools to help patch things up for the moment. I've had the most success with the following process in preparing for competition. During the warm-up, I leave the bridle in a normal position. A few moments before entering the ring I tighten the noseband and flash to restrict the tongue. Be careful not to make it too tight. In no way am I advocating tightening the bridle in such a way that your horse cannot move his jaw. It's not intended to be a cruel solution. (You also must remember that in dressage you can be eliminated from the competition if the judge deems the noseband too tight.)

CAUTION: Care must be taken here—don't make the noseband too tight and, certainly, don't try it for the first time at a show. I simulate the experience at home, so that if something does start to go wrong you have an option to fix it.

It is important to leave yourself five minutes or so to finish warming up. I've made the mistake of tightening the bridle literally just before entering the ring, which resulted in a tense horse for the first few movements of the dressage test.

I.2 Simon is modeling a correctly fitted Crescent noseband. Note that the metal portion should be in contact with his upper and lower jaw without pinching his lip between it and the bit.

Solution D

There is another option that was initially intended to fix the next problem on the list (see p. 80): a Crescent (or half-moon) noseband (fig. I.2). The noseband contains a half-moon piece of metal that starts above the bit, curves in front, and finishes below the bit. There are four attachments of leather to the metal portion: At the top it attaches to a strap that goes over the poll to determine how high or low the noseband sits; a second strap attaches above and behind the nose; the third strap attaches over the nose; and the last strap attaches below the bit. I've had some success using it to break the tongue habit. It works by physically blocking the tongue from coming out of the mouth.

Solution E

Check to make sure the bridle fits correctly, and falls within the horse's preference. Play around with the cheek pieces that establish the height of the bit. Some horses prefer the bit set lower, while others higher. Along the same

A Learning Experience

A few years back I had a horse that was quite a good mover, not an outwardly nervous type in the least. However, he had an awful habit of putting his tongue out of the left side of his mouth. Unfortunately, it wasn't just peeking out, but hanging out like a Labrador's—one that has been chasing a ball for hour in the summer heat! We tried everything we could think of: adjusted the bridle, bit location, bit type, Crescent noseband. The only thing that had any sort of effect was the tension of the noseband. When set loosely, his tongue hung like the dog's, but when tightened within reason, it would stay in his mouth for a few minutes. He also was responsive to a light tug on the left rein: After each tug, he'd stick it back inside for a few strides.

So our plan for dressage competition became clear. The strategy was as follows:

During the warm-up, we'd continue as if there wasn't an issue. About two minutes before entering the ring, we'd tighten the noseband, as well as the flash. This would buy us a little time without the tongue hanging out. The real trick came while riding the test in the arena. If I were heading straight toward the judge I wouldn't worry about the tongue, but every time I passed the short side on the right rein, I'd make a few quick tugs on the rein as I was approaching the quarterline. This allowed me to remain extremely soft between quarterlines: Seeing that he'd generally stick his tongue out with a contact, I could effectively hide his tongue from the judge with this plan. While not 100 percent perfect, it worked to a degree. He consistently scored very well, placing above where I expected he'd be after that first ride.

theme, try different bit diameters. Again some horses prefer thinner versus thicker bits, as well as single versus double-jointed mouthpieces.

Crossing the Jaw and Grabbing the Bit to Bolt

What Happens

A horse crosses his jaw to lock on one rein or the other; once he has a good hold on it, you're going for a wild ride while he uses you for balance.

This is another habit prevalent in ex-racehorses. Generally, it occurs when galloping on cross-country; cantering out of or into the ring; and in downward transitions. When you try to slow down or rebalance your horse, he will "cross his jaw," that is, his lower jaw opens and is displaced sideways. He does this in order to lock on to the bit, which allows him to pull with a much stronger force than he could otherwise.

▶ Cause One

The horse has an underlying misunderstanding of contact and how to properly rebalance himself. Instead of using his hindquarters to carry the majority of his weight, he relies on the rider as a "fifth leg" for support in order to maintain his balance. If the rider can manage to drop the contact, the horse will be forced to figure out another way to stay on his feet. The trick is to complete the downward transition without pulling!

Solution A

Although the problem seems to be most severe in the open or in a large arena, the solution lies in flatwork. I start off doing a lot of transitions, both between gaits as well as within gaits. Seeing that your horse will be looking for any chance to lock on to the contact, your problem is very similar to the horse that grabs the reins (see p. 68). This horse just takes it one step farther: Once the rider is jostled loose, he quickly accelerates.

You'll need to start at "square one" with this horse because there is a fundamental hole in his training. He doesn't know how to use his body properly to perform a downward transition. Along with the misunderstanding, it has now become a habit. So even if you show him the correct way, it will take a while to remap the pathways in his brain to a new normal.

Exercise

1 Get to work on the ground again with your longeing equipment, and with the rubber donut or solid side-reins. Once the horse is longeing competently, you can do the real work. You begin with countless transitions.

2 Start with a trot-to-walk transition. As you ask him to perform the downward transition, his first response will be to lock on to the side-reins. You must be very quick with your response: The moment you see a shift in balance, where he starts to rely on the side-reins, you must again send him forward, and at the same time, give him a quick sharp tug on the longe line.

The goal is to make it clear to the horse that even in the downward transition he must use his hindquarters to support his weight and not your hand. The first few times you make this correction he may go back into the trot. Don't get mad about this—he is simply trying different responses trying to figure out what you're looking for. Once back in the trot, prepare and ask for the walk again, keeping a watchful eye on the contact and hindquarter engagement.

3 The moment he goes to grab the bit, point the whip toward his hindquarters with a quick supportive rein aid. Again, the shift of balance should be evident, so ask again for the walk. As this goes on, you'll start to ask for the downward transition closer and closer to the rebalancing aid. Soon enough you'll get a well-balanced trot-to-walk transition.

4 Take the same steps for canter to trot, and trot to walk and when these are accomplished, start to introduce the same concept *within* a gait. For example, at a canter, the average horse makes approximately 16 strides for a 20-meter circle, or 8 strides per half circle. Ask for a lengthening with more conviction in your voice and taking the driving stance. You should be able to reduce the strides in his half circle from the normal 8 down to 7—or less.

5 The same should be true when collecting the canter. Take a less aggressive stance, make quicker half-halts, and increase the number of strides to 9 or more on the half circle. The actual number is not terribly important, but it gives you a quantitative method to evaluate your success.

6 In addition to lengthening and shortening the stride on a fixed circle, you can spiral in and out.

Solution B

Another great tool to help your horse understand this concept is longeing with the use of poles or cavalletti.

Exercise

1 Either put the poles on a different diameter circle, or start to work on an oval (Diagram 2). I've had great luck with five or more trot poles placed at the top of an oval.

2 Start off the exercise at a canter and establish a good canter on a circle. Now, ask for the trot on the long portion of the oval so that the moment he drops into the trot, he is stepping over the first trot pole. It is very difficult at this point for him to lock on the bit and fall forward due to the simple fact that he has to stay on his feet.

Longeing should become an integral part of this horse's daily routine, until all of these exercises are easily accomplished. Very much like working with him for the first time, you're looking to expand his vocabulary of sorts; once this is learned, it should be easier to translate when riding.

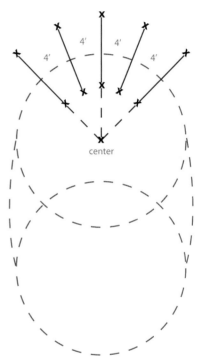

Diagram 2

Poles on a circle: The dotted lines can be on any diameter but the distance from the center of the each rail to the next should be 4 feet. The easiest way to set up is to mark the center of the circle and walk the radius. This will insure you have a round circle.

Solution C

Assuming you've accomplished both Solution A and B, hop on and get going.

Exercise

1 Start with the same progression you used when longeing. Working from a trot, ask for a walk. Depending on his level of education it wouldn't hurt to also use your voice when giving an aid until it is confirmed in your horse's mind. He will probably lock on the bit again, so very much like when longeing, quickly use a firm supportive rein while giving him a sharp kick with your leg. The duration of this combined aid is the most important factor. It should be nearly *instant*, that is, as soon as it begins, it's ended. You can be very firm with your hand and leg, just make sure it doesn't last long enough for your horse to adjust and lock on. If he does—you're sunk!

This is one of the most difficult tasks: It's just so easy to start off with a light contact, half-halt, then soften to a slightly heavier contact. As this sequence continues, the horse will get heavier over time. So make sure when you release, you release back to your starting contact point.

In addition to a sharp aid, you can also help break the lock he has on your reins by increasing the bend. The more he locks, the more bend you should create, and the moment he unlocks, straighten him back out.

2 At this point you've got your transitions between gaits going consistently well. Now move onto transitions within the gait. Counting strides on a circle or straight line is a great way to evaluate your success (see p. 81); I would also add in some cavalletti or raised rails to add a bit more difficulty.

Solution D

If you are working with an event horse, then out in the field you go. But before getting there, make sure you can go from a canter to a hand gallop to an outright gallop and back to canter without trouble. If so, you've graduated to the field! Take your horse out on a hack, and find a field that you can use. Preferably, it's a place where you can use the entire field rather than just the perimeter.

The idea is to continue this gradual progression. Start when you're warming up on a circle. Expect the same level of responses that you got in the ring. If this isn't the case, you'll be in the field for the foreseeable future. Some horses get very excited about being in a strange environment. This field has to become commonplace so I would head back every day for your flatwork—and jumping if possible—until he is no different in the field than in the ring.

Once you have control on a circle in the field, start to open this circle to an oval where the long sides become longer and longer until you have an indefinite straight line—where you never lose control and can add a half-circle without difficulty. On this straight line, if you ever feel the horse start to shift his balance forward and grab the bit, instantly enter into a circle: You should have the upper hand on the bend. From this point, start to add some jumps; again, the moment you lose control you're on that circle in an instant. It may end up that you are jumping a log on a 20-meter circle for the entire day. If that's the case, so be it. You have to be more patient and committed than your horse.

Bitting Solution

"What about bitting?" you may well ask. As you may have figured out by now, I'm not a big bit person. Of the twenty-plus horses I'm currently competing, the strongest bit in use is a twisted snaffle. Most people will instantly say, "Well, you are just stronger than me!" Personally, I can't stand horses that pull or hang on the rein. I'm all for a featherlight contact regardless of the discipline.

You can certainly try some more severe bits than a standard snaffle. The bit has to be strong enough so that you are able to make an impact if needed, but I'd try to keep to the most forgiving one you can manage. During jumping combinations and options where you need to turn, it'll benefit you most to have a soft horse that is round and pliable.

Stronger bits have the effect of creating a less steady connection, which makes it very difficult to maintain a soft, consistent contact throughout a course or a test. Go to a local show, and watch the people riding with the "biggest" bits. Ninety-nine percent of the time they will be the ones verging on being out of control. The horse is too busy fighting the bit to real-

tip *Another consideration: Let the horse gallop! With an event horse, especially, it's very important not to hang on him when galloping. He should gallop as if he's on cruise control. You should set the pace and balance and he should maintain it indefinitely—and most importantly, on a light-to-loose contact.*

On a cross-country course, there are 20 to 30 times where you need your horse's undivided attention. These are the jumping efforts! The last thing you want to do is nag him where you use up his attention span in the first 15 jumps because you've been "messing" with him all the time he's galloping between jumps. Leave him alone!

You are looking to foster an independent-thinking horse that only needs you to steer him in the right direction. He should ideally be in a good balance and pace by himself.

I.3 As on p. 78, a Crescent noseband is used here, too, but in a different way. As Simon begins to cross his jaw, the metal sides help to prevent anything more than "minimal" crossing.

ize fully what's being asked of him, often resulting in run-outs, stops, or nappy behavior.

Bridle Solution

Aside from bitting, there is another option that has helped me in the past with horses like this. It is the Crescent noseband (fig. I.3). I made a quick mention of it in the Tongue Issues discussion (p. 75). Seeing that it's metal and wraps from the top of the bit to the bottom, it has the ability to prevent the horse from crossing his jaw. How tight you make it depends a lot on the horse, but you probably want to get it about as tight as you can for it to work best. Some horses will instantly respond to it by not crossing their jaw, while others will improve but not all the way. I've not had a horse yet that didn't get at least a little bit better by using the Crescent. I'd go shopping if I were you!

Strong Horses or "Pullers"

What Happens

The horse leans on your reins and is just dull and unresponsive to your aids. This is usually a learned behavior, although some horses are predisposed at birth to pull.

Most commonly seen when jumping, a strong horse is a little like the horse that crosses his jaw and locks onto the bit (see p. 80). This problem, however, is slightly different in that a purely strong horse will effectively be duller in the mouth than most, and unfortunately, unlike for the horse that crosses his jaw, there isn't an instant fix to resolve the issue.

▶ Cause One

Some horses—like people—are born more sensitive than others. Generally, your classic puller is one that is not all that sensitive and has learned to rely on the rider for support.

Solution A

Transitions and many of the same exercises already covered will help a strong horse. Seeing that he is generally dull to your hand, it's important to teach him to be more responsive to your other aids. Your weight is probably the most under-utilized aid: Pay close attention and don't allow your upper body to lean forward because this tends to place your horse more on the forehand, furthering his need to hang on you.

Solution B

The horse that pulls is the one type I'd say to go ahead and become creative with your bitting options. Many strong horses can be very bold and quick jump-ers. It is without doubt a safety issue when you can't get them sufficiently slowed down before a jump or combination.

As I've already said, I don't like to use anything very severe in a horse's mouth, but I've had great luck making a combination bridle with a hacka-more and adding a bit. This allows for more stopping power that can be easily released. It's also adjustable on the fly. You can always soften the hackamore rein if the combination seems like overkill.

A few cautions here: although hackamores are great, and generally work very well, their effect does wear off over time. I wouldn't use one except in competition once you're convinced it's the right option; the more you use it, the less effective it becomes. The beauty of this "combination system" is that the hackamore works like an emergency brake. It gets you stopped in a hurry, but with a bit that is not too severe, you can also turn easily without a fight. It generally produces a better "shape" (bascule) over the jump, and when you are on course, it's very easy to increase or decrease how much bit to use on the fly.

There is also a custom-made bit called the Hackabit, which as the name suggests, is a combination bit that contains both actions. It is popular in the show-jumping world and can produce good results. However, on a cross-country course a horse cannot be steered quite as well with one as he can in a normal bit. For this reason, you might be better off making your own combination bridle.

The easiest way I've found to put this combination together is to use a strap that is made for a double bridle that you can feed through the browband over the horse's head and down the other side. This suspends the hackamore and allows the bridle and bit to be in a normal configuration. I like to use a curb rein (thin leather rein without stops) for the hackamore, so that if you slip or lose your reins and have to quickly grab them in an effort to regain control, the snaffle rein will tend to "catch" on your glove first. This will decrease the likelihood of your pulling on the hackamore rein alone. When you have to turn tightly, you don't want to grab the hackamore rein.

Along with the combination bits, gags or three-ring bits will often do the trick. Generally, a gag gets a horse lighter with his nose out. A three-ring bit helps a strong horse that pulls, but it can create a "curling" neck shape where he ends up behind the vertical. Be creative: Try a number of bits. You'll begin to see general trends, but remember, every horse is different.

CAUTION: When dealing with the type of horse that pulls and considering what bit to try, bear in mind the horse will probably become less sensitive to a bit over time. So when you find one that works well, keep it packed in your trailer for shows only! If you use it every day it will soon lose its effectiveness..

Solution C

It is vitally important that you teach horses, and especially strong horses, to respond promptly to your weight shift. In order to teach this, set up a double bounce 12 feet apart (three jumps set 12 feet apart) in the center of your ring.

Pick up a hand gallop around the outside of your arena. This is solely to get him on a longer and maybe slightly strung-out balance. Then make a gradual turn to approach the bounces (within four strides). At the same time, open your hip angle from a full two-point seat to a very light three-point seat along with a gentle increase in rein pressure. The first time through, your horse will probably be going just a tick too quickly and feel as if the combination is too tight. Again, get your hand gallop and repeat the process. Most horses will quickly figure out that when you shift your weight back they should slow down and shift their balance.

Once your horse successfully jumps through the bounce exercise, move on to a combination, which finishes with a bounce exercise. In competition, many times you will see a triple bar then four-to-six strides into a combination, or set short to a narrow, tall vertical. The course designer has included this exercise to confirm that your horse is "adjustable" and that he doesn't take flight following the triple bar and run through the second jump. This can be a challenge, especially when you're riding a strong, or careless, horse!

To prepare your horse, set up the following exercise (Diagram 3). This combination initially is set 64 feet from the triple bar to the bounces. The triple bar will allow you to ride at a slightly stronger pace than a vertical or square oxer would; it also creates a flatter bascule over the fence, which sets your horse up for a learning experience at the bounces.

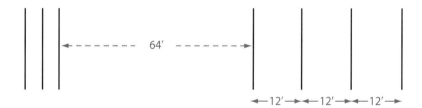

Diagram 3

This exercise, a combination of a triple jump finishing with bounces, is designed to stretch or lengthen the horse's stride, then in response to the rider's weight, shorten it. The second half of the combination helps the horse to understand that your weight transfer is a warning that the upcoming jumps may be short. This is the basic configuration. Keep in mind that set in an open field, the 64-foot distance will be easier to cover than when set in an arena. Don't be afraid to tweak the distance so that your horse has to be ridden forward to the first jump, then has to make a moderate effort to rebalance when reaching the bounces.

The goal is to jump into the line with enough pace so the horse may be inclined to get slightly strung out and strong. The distance of 64 feet is 4 feet longer than the "ideal" distance. Within the last two strides before the first bounce, open your hip angle, shift your weight back, apply a slight amount of constant rein pressure and allow the remaining bounces to do the rest. Once through the exercise a few times, your horse will feel your weight transfer and immediately begin to rebalance himself. If your horse jumps through with ease, you can increase the level of difficulty by stretching the distance between the first two jumps. This will force you to ride with more pace into the triple bar, and subsequently you'll have to collect and rebalance more to successfully jump through the bounces.

In an ideal world, even on a strong horse, you should be able to gallop on with very little to no rein contact supporting him. But, when you shift your weight back and open your hip angle, your horse should respond by rebalancing, readying himself for the upcoming jump.

Solution D

Horses that appear strong can actually be quite weak. Their fitness plan is vital. As your horse becomes physically fitter, he will become lighter—that is, less strong. Hills are your best friend. If you are lucky enough to have a hill nearby, go out and work on it at least twice a week.

When you're trying to increase a horse's strength, canter poles can be tremendously beneficial. Start with spacing them farther apart and gradually move them closer to teach him to compress and support his own body. At a canter, for example, you should start at 8 feet apart; then you can realistically work all the way down to 3 feet. It will take time, but horses are capable of amazing things: Our Intermediate and Advanced-level eventers can canter through trot poles without a problem!

▶ Cause Two

Because of a lack of balance, a horse often starts to pull and uses the rider for support.

Solution

Take advantage of a ground person—or a mirror, if available in the arena—to determine if your horse is truly straight or not. Many horses turn their body into a "pretzel" with their haunches in and their shoulder "popping" out. This lack of straightness inevitably creates a very unstable position where the rider ends up supporting the horse's weight. Performing many straightening and suppling exercises will be of help. Try to build a horizontal pyramid: The horse's hips are the widest portion of his body so they act as the foundation; centered and above them are the horse's shoulders; and centered on top of the shoulders is the poll. When one component is displaced to one side or the other, the entire structure falls down. Don't allow yourself to hold a crooked pyramid together with your reins. When you get your horse's body aligned, you will be able to finally sit back and relax.

Unruly Outbursts

For the lack of a better term, "unruly outbursts" will cover a number of behaviors, tricks, and ploys your horse may use to get out of work, or worse yet, get rid of you! All of these problems can often be stamped out in short order as long as you are vigilant and "grab them by the horns." Most horses will give up all of these games once they realize that they are just wasted energy.

Rearing

What Happens

The horse rocks back and balances on his hind legs, while his front end comes off the ground. A horse rears in order to evade something. Whether he is trying to intimidate the rider or is scared of a situation, he stands on his hind end.

Rearing is one of the most dangerous behavioral issues you'll encounter. It's a behavior used by the horse either to intimidate a rider or avoid a frightening object or situation in his path.

First, when used as intimidation and the rider (whom I do not blame) then backs off, the horse has won! He has now trained the rider: When the horse is asked to do something he doesn't want to

II.I A-F A rearing sequence showing Crown Talisman's ("Tali's") progression of movement. Throughout, I'm trying my best to keep my hips slightly in front of my shoulders. This prevents me from getting ahead of the motion and allows me to positively influence what is happening rather than struggling for my balance as my horse attempts to maintain his.

do, he can rear and the rider releases pressure thus allowing him to continue doing what he likes. Second, rearing when the horse is scared may precede him bolting: Remember that horses are creatures of flight, so the sensitive ones that want to get out of an uncomfortable situation as quickly as possible can rear. In both cases, your horse will often use the rear to spin 180 degrees. The general progression of a rear is as follows:

CAUTION: The consequence of less-than-optimal timing when applying aids during a rear can result in serious injury to you and your horse. So, if you have any reservations whatsoever, please consult a local professional for help.

1 Your horse "drops behind your leg." By this, I mean he goes from a forward-thinking "feel" to one where he feels as if he's just dropped into neutral; or worse yet, the parking brake has been applied (fig. II.1 A).

2 He will start to drop one shoulder and take the opposing rein (e. g. drop the left shoulder and take hold of the right rein).

3 You will feel his front end slightly drop and begin to turn (fig. II.1 B).

4 Next, the rear begins in earnest. His front end lifts off the ground (fig. II.1 C).

5 The rear will continue to elevate until reaching the apex. You'll feel a momentary pause at the apex, then his front end returns to the ground (figs. II.1 D & E).

6 The horse will bolt, rear again, or continue as if nothing has happened (fig. II.1 F).

Rearing has many causes: Some horses learn to rear as an evasion to avoid going forward or maintaining contact. Others begin to rear because they are nappy, barn sour or herd bound. For this chapter, I'll discuss how to deal with the behavior itself rather than the trigger, which I will cover later (p. 116).

▶ **Cause One**
Some horses resort to rearing due to mouth pain or discomfort.

Solution

I mentioned it earlier in Section I on Contact Issues, but I want to reiterate here that you should have a dentist check the horse's mouth before going further with a horse that rears. It's best to rule out any physical issues that may be contributing to the problem at hand before attempting any of the solutions that follow.

▶ Cause Two

I would also caution those who use Happy Mouth plastic-covered bits to check them carefully each time you ride. I've had bad luck in the past with them becoming very sharp—they are pliable enough to come apart after being chewed.

Solution

See my discussion of Happy Mouth bits (p. 66).

▶ Cause Three

Rearing can have many triggers, but the action on the horse's part is always the same. Once the trigger has been "pressed," whether a deer jumping out in front of you or simply your horse does not want to go forward, he will quickly lift his front end off the ground and finish up standing on his hindquarters.

tip *This is a good time to discuss the two types of horses that exhibit this type of behavior. Personally, I will only deal with the first type—the horse that has some sense of self-preservation even though he may exhibit all sorts of bad behavior. He's the type that approaches a fence, rock, or anything that might endanger him, and stops in order not to injure himself.*

The second type is the horse that will do anything as an evasion, including injuring himself. He doesn't care if he kills himself in the process of trying to get you off. This horse is not one worth riding—ever.

Where do you draw the line? I like to think that if I'm riding a horse, he too does not want to get hurt. If he backs up or runs into an object more than once, I'd seriously consider looking for another horse. Your health is worth it, be conservative. The sidebar on p. 95 details just one example of a horse I decided was better off in a field than in my ring.

Solution A

Dealing with a rearing horse requires the rider to have extraordinary balance and timing. As the horse lifts his front end off the ground you need to stay in balance. For this to happen, your body should remain perpendicular to the ground; the higher the horse goes up, the closer your upper body will be to his neck—very much like riding up a steep hill. If you have to err on one side or the other, you'd rather be *too far forward*, that is, hugging the neck. If you get caught leaning back, *do not pull on the reins for balance*—especially during Step 5 of the rearing progression (see p. 93)! When you've lost your balance and use the reins for support, you are likely to pull your horse back and over on top of you. Should you happen to feel yourself falling, your best bet is to bail out. As hard as that may seem it's the better of the two unenviable options you have at the moment. You're much better off landing on the ground alone than with your 1,200-pound friend on top of you.

A Learning Experience

A number of years ago we had a three-year-old that was in our barn to start. She had an incredibly quick rear. It had begun with a previous rider and I was asked to hop on and see what I could do with her. I had never been on such a horse. With virtually no warning, she would rear with such ferocity that she'd fully rotate and land on her back. (Usually, when a horse flips over once, he doesn't flip again.)

This mare would flip repeatedly—not bothered a bit. The first time she went up, I found myself instantly on my back with her landing on me. I was very lucky that she didn't land squarely on me, but off to the right on my thigh. The tree of my saddle actually broke on my leg. After a few minutes I did get back on, but I was not riding for a few weeks due to a leg that was purple with a swelling the size of an apple on its inside.

When I eventually got back on, I rode without stirrups. She would begin to rear, I'd bail, and she'd land on her back. After a day of this happening repeatedly, I decided there are times you must cut your losses and move on to a different horse. It's not worth getting hurt.

II.2 A-D In A, Tali is both rearing and bolting to my left. I'm doing my best to open my right rein to increase the right bend. Photo B is such an awkward photo, but it clearly shows what effect my opening rein is having. The lock in his neck is nearly broken, and I'm beginning to feel as if I have the upper hand. Then, success! In C we're back on the ground with a right bend established. He doesn't look particularly pleased. We head back in the correct direction in D!

Solution B

Keep in mind that a horse will usually will give you some warning before the rear happens (see Step 1 of the rearing progression, p. 93). Once these signs are identified there are a few key tools that can help.

Exercise

1 I can't stress enough how critical your timing is when fixing a rearing horse. Your goal is to identify the rear as it is about to occur and quickly use an *opening* *inside rein* with as much force as you can manage. (Generally you'd be heading in one direction just preceding the rear, in which case your *inside* rein is clear. And when on a straight line, 99 percent of the time you are working to push the horse left or right...again it's clear. But when it's not, then I generally pull to my dominant hand.) And, you want to implement the following aids between Steps 2 and 4 or after Step 5 of the rearing progression (see p. 93).

2 It is very important to use an *opening rein*, which should be at least 12 inches to the outside of where your hand is normally positioned, effectively above your knee or even farther to the outside: 12 inches is the minimum distance—more is better in this case. As the horse begins to rear he will try to lock his neck in a straight line, and most times, grab hold of the bit.

3 The opening rein serves two proposes. First, it breaks the lock he has in his neck, and you can get the upper hand when you can establish a bend. Second, the opening rein initiates a turn that will disturb the horse's balance so he won't be stable enough to stand up on his hind end (figs. II.2 A–D).

4 Once you've initiated the opening rein, your leg must instantly follow—it should occur nearly simultaneously. When you apply force to your rein the horse will begin the process of bending and your leg is used firmly to accelerate the bend through his body, and to make sure the horse does not fall onto the inside shoulder. If he falls in, he is better able to grab that *inside rein* again.

tip *You have to be very careful when dealing with a rear: If you are even a moment too late with your application of rein aids, your horse may remain locked in his neck, and the increased rein pressure will actually accelerate the rate at which he's rearing. He'll be standing on his hind end before you can even blink.*

5 As the horse begins to yield from your leg and hand pressure, he'll start to lose his balance and his front feet will return to earth. Once on the ground he should continue the turn you asked for while in the rear. If you're able to keep him turning, you need to soften your inside rein and ride him forward in a small circle and progressively spiral out. You are looking to increase the bend through his body without getting too much bend in his head and neck. The spiraling should be driven by your inside leg, with the outside rein preventing too much bend and his "popping" the outside shoulder.

6 When his feet get higher than 6 inches off the ground, it's too late to use an opening rein. Your window of opportunity has closed and you need to transition to flip-prevention mode. You must, at this point, release any pressure you had on the reins until the horse reaches his highest point in the rear. Just like a ball being thrown up in the air, he will get higher quickly, and just like the ball, he will slow and pause at his maximum elevation. When this point is reached, it's now safe for you to use as much opening *inside rein* as you can muster.

7 The goal is to break that lock in his neck before his front feet hit the ground and have a chance to go up again. This is the safest part of the rear: On the way down you can be as aggressive as you like with the inside rein and leg. When you can break this lock, you're in great shape.

Solution C

Once you've fixed the first rear encountered, your goal must shift to prevention of future rears. Good riding is defined by your ability to anticipate what is going to happen next, and begin to fix the problem before it arises. Horses are creatures of habit; they generally act in a consistent manner when in a similar situation. Look for the trigger that seems to lead this horse to rear. Once you've identified this precursor, maybe more than one, start using lateral exercises to your advantage. Many times you'll feel him drop his shoulder, or begin to suck back. Treat these instances seriously; they are an indicator of what is coming next!

Exercise

Ride in a circle just outside the area where the rear usually begins and start to spiral out of the circle toward the trigger spot: You should be getting closer and closer to it each time around the circle. Continue this process for as long as you are able to maintain the bend, which prevents your horse from grabbing the inside rein. When you reach the limit, stay there until you can keep him soft. Once he is consistently soft, move one track closer until you're passing just next to the trigger point.

Bucking

What Happens

A buck is a motion the horse does in the air as if he is jumping an imaginary fence. He can also add a little extra kick at the tail end of the "jump." The horse often "takes" the reins as he jumps his front end up, followed by kicking his hind end up into the air.

When he bucks, the game the horse is playing is to unseat or, at least, inflict a blow to the rider's confidence by forcing her to back off. Once the horse has exposed this weakness, he is free to do as he likes: anything from larger bucks, to simply refusing to move forward. Bucking is a strange, "funny" behavior. It can either strike fear into riders, or make them burst into uncontrollable laughter.

On the pages that follow, I'm going to discuss bucking, which I break down into three main categories: the *Happy Bucker* (Cause One, p. 101); two types of the *Malicious Bucker* (Causes Two and Three, pp. 102 and 103); and the *Cold-Backed Bucker* (Cause Four, p. 106). However it begins, the same method of dealing with bucking applies to all three types: *Get the horse's head up!*

Tack and Equipment

Before I get to the causes and solutions to your horse's bucking problem, there are a few items of equipment and some tack adjustments that can make you a much more effective rider.

I've always found it easier to remain in a secure position with shorter stirrups. You should select a saddle with a relatively flat seat—I prefer my jumping saddle for a horse that is known to buck. The flatter seat and shorter stirrups allow you to get out of the tack and "hover" above the horse's back. He then can buck or gyrate as much as he'd like below—and independent—of you. As I mentioned before, if you can imagine a buck as being like a horse jumping a large fence, it's usually not the takeoff that's a problem; it's the landing portion that "gets" people!

Longer stirrups and dressage saddles that make you "wrap" around the horse will end up working against you, especially when you have a very athletic horse underneath. The higher his hind end goes up, the farther forward the

Prevent a Buck: Two Rules to Live By

First is "Heads Up"! Both of you: horse and rider. When your head and eyes go down so will your upper body, and you'll find yourself just where you were looking—on the ground! As for your horse, he won't be able to buck when his head is up. Keep his poll at the highest point, period. No excuses. Use whatever means necessary (figs. II.3 A–G).

The second rule is "Go Forward"! Ninety-nine percent of buckers are bucking to get out of work, and a horse is better able to buck when he is behind your leg. The moment your horse even thinks about responding sluggishly off your leg, you must get after him. This means add your leg lightly. When he doesn't respond as he should, ask again with the same light force, and decisively use your whip.

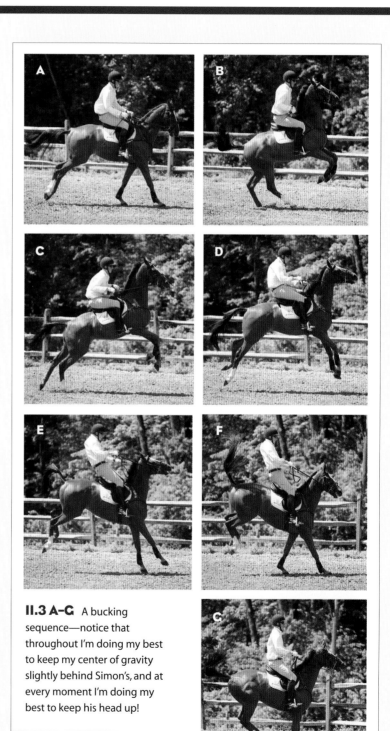

II.3 A–G A bucking sequence—notice that throughout I'm doing my best to keep my center of gravity slightly behind Simon's, and at every moment I'm doing my best to keep his head up!

saddle pushes your body. You're going to spend most of your time trying to rebalance yourself instead of correcting your horse.

Many people also use a yoke or neck strap to allow for a little more security in time of need.

Aside from this tack, I also like to use a dressage whip. It has a larger impact and longer reach than your short jumping bat, but the key again here is to actively try to get his head up and use your whip simultaneously. The whip will allow you to keep hold of the reins throughout.

Self-Test

Before going further into the causes and solutions for buckers, I'm going to introduce a short self-examination test here. For this, I'm going to assume that your horse (or another) has bucked before so you are somewhat familiar with the feeling. You have two options:

First, when your horse bucked and you stuck with him like a bareback bronc rider, please read the sidebar on p. 100 and then follow my solutions.

Second, if your horse has managed to buck you off or has found a way to intimidate you, I want you to confirm to yourself that you are 100 percent committed to fixing this problem. Keep in mind that during the process, there are some horses whose resolve may be stronger than yours. There is no shame in hiring a professional, and I can assure you, it makes your life significantly less stressful and probably safer.

tip *In general, when training horses you have to allow them to be themselves. They may land off a jump and buck or just randomly give off a small buck. I never want to completely squelch their personality. I see training as more of an effort to guide them to be better, but not to lose their personal flair.*

Think about it: When you have a leaking faucet in your house, I'm sure you could read about how to fix it, but you will probably call a plumber in anyway (and this faucet isn't going to plant you on the ground!)

So for those of you committed to fixing the bucking problem yourself, let's get to it!

▶ Cause One: *The Happy Bucker*

The first category of horse exhibiting this behavior can be classified as the *Happy Bucker*. You see this when a horse is feeling good, often following the first jump of the day or the first canter in a field. Ninety-nine percent of the time he is just showing that he is enjoying life. Not that this is a good habit to form, but, in this case, I'm not terribly strict or harsh in my correction.

Solution

Most horses that buck are *behind* your leg, in other words, they are not being responsive enough to your forward aids. As long as it's not dangerous, I gently lift his head at the same time that I apply my leg, asking him to move on. Of course, there is a line to be crossed where bucking becomes obnoxious, and I escalate my response to limit it.

You would always rather have your horse's head too high than too low.

▶ **Cause Two: *The Malicious Bucker—Type One***
Ultimately, for this horse, bucking is just a means to unseat the rider.

Solution

You need to be aggressive! When in doubt about your horse's intentions, your riding position needs to be defensive with your upper body back and your center of gravity behind your horse's center of gravity. If your upper body gets pulled forward, you're in deep trouble! With your shoulders back, your lower leg should be anchored with your heels down and well in front of you.

You are going to correct the buck by accomplishing two main goals: The first is to get his head up with whatever means possible. When it is up, it's nearly impossible for him to buck. At the same time, you're going to use your whip to assist your leg in driving him forward.

Pay attention to where the horse is going: When he is bucking and heading toward a jump or the rail around the arena, he is likely to spin or turn before running into it.

Riding the Bucking Horse

My eyes are constantly switching between where I want to go and the bridle's crown piece on a horse that is known to buck, but I don't look any lower than his poll. I'm sure you've been told to keep your eyes straight ahead or on the horizon. However, my problem with this advice becomes apparent on the horse that is likely to buck (or rear and spin). In most cases, you get an indication of which direction he is planning to turn by watching his ears. This split second of information can be critical for maintaining your balance. At all costs, don't let your shoulders get in front of your hips!

▶ **Cause Two:** *The Malicious Bucker—Type Two*

This horse may be bucking not necessarily to get you off but to either intimidate or reduce the effectiveness of the rider. Would you describe your horse as "behind your leg"? Does he normally buck after you ask him to move more forward?

Solution A

Exercise

1 Start with a halt-to-walk transition. Walking gives you the best shot to regain the upper hand. With your leg, lightly ask him to walk forward and if he doesn't respond, or he responds very slowly, use your whip to reinforce your leg aids. Lay down the law by making sure your initial reaction is very clear and that the consequences to him are great. You can always give your horse love pats and treats from then on.

2 Ask your horse to move promptly off into the walk from the halt. He will probably try to drop his head, swish his tail and round his back. So, give him a very stern, quick "pop" on the rein at the same time you use your leg and whip.

3 A decisive pop is necessary seeing that you would be pulled out of the saddle if you tried to give him a progressive half-halt. You can't be too strong at this moment. You might say, "It would hurt Snoopy, though." GOOD! It had better. Snoopy is trying to lay your butt in the sand!

4 Once your horse jumps into the walk with the lightest leg aid—that is, becomes in "front of your leg"—you can move on to the trot. Repeat the same process that you did in the halt to walk: Ask for the trot from the walk, also trot from halt. Both transitions should improve his responsiveness to your leg. If he does manage to buck, you have to instantly get your shoulders back with yours leg solidly out in front of you, and correct him just the same way as you did in the halt-to-walk transition.

✳ **tip** *Don't be afraid to use your whip. Correcting a horse in the right way is a decisive, forceful action that lasts indefinitely. When you are "weak," and just give him a "love tap," you'll be repeating this same "tapping" to fix the problem for as long as you own him. Just think about how you would feel if you were being nagged incessantly every day and all you had to look forward to was being hit countless times every day. Not so excited or motivated to work, right?*

5 At this point, you should have the halt-walk-trot down pat and your horse is very prompt to react to any aid to go forward. So, let's move on to the canter. This canter is the most precarious gait in that he can buck easily with every step. All he has to do is plant and jump with his hind legs—and the opportunity is there every stride for this to occur. The goal is to establish in your horse's mind that you'll win no matter what happens and to convince him that he doesn't

Using the Whip

How do you effectively use your whip? Here are two methods:

Reins in One Hand

I prefer this method when using a crop and use it when at all possible with a horse that is bucking. It is significantly more effective if you can use your entire arm strength to make contact rather than just your wrist (described in the second method on p. 105). Practice taking both reins in one hand, until it is second nature so that you don't even think about it in the time of need. It should just happen.

I am right-handed, so naturally I prefer to use the crop in my right hand. However, you should practice holding it in either hand so that if needed, you can switch. For this exercise, we'll assume you're holding the crop in your right hand.

1 While holding your reins correctly, move both hands closer together, rotating your right hand so that the slack of rein coming out of your hand near your thumb can easily be picked up by your left hand (figs. II.4 A–D).

II.4 A–D In Photo A, I am holding the reins in a half-bridge. My left rein is held as normal and the right rein is between my middle and ring finger. I still have slight contact with the right rein in B, but this rein is secured at this point in my left hand. In C my right hand is free, and I still have quite good lateral control with my left hand and both reins. Photo D shows the other option, which is much less effective as a driving aid, but allows for much better steering. I have an opening rein on the right, enough that my crop can still make contact without hitting my leg.

2 As they get close, open the thumb of your left hand so that you can grasp the slack and not completely lose contact with the left rein.

3 Once it is secured by your left hand, raise your right hand and quickly strike by moving down and back in an effort to make the whip come into contact with the horse's hindquarters.

want to mess with you! Make sure you have an active trot where he is nearly cantering on his own given that he has so much energy. Ask for the canter, and mean it! If he doesn't canter right away, use your whip and sit back. He has to go forward at all costs. Once in the canter, your goal is to establish a very forward active canter that isn't "running," but you can, initially, err on the side of doing a too-forward rather than a slow canter.

4 When you are expecting to have to use the whip, I expedite this process by riding with a half-bridge, that is, the slack of your right rein is placed in the left hand. This process will allow you to be a fraction quicker with your whip and eliminate the possibility of dropping the rein.

Reins in Two Hands

If you feel that removing your hand from the rein might create a dangerous situation, you can use a dressage whip without taking your hand away (figs. II.5 A & B). This has the distinct advantage of allowing complete control of both reins, which gives you a tremendous advantage with a horse that is trying to spin, run out at a jump, or spook.

I When striking the horse, you must make sure you're not giving conflicting aids. It's very important that you're not driving the horse and holding him at the same time. You do this best by opening your whip hand so as you rotate your wrist, your hand is far enough to the outside to not make contact with your thigh.

II.5 A & B This pair of photos shows the same two-rein technique but with a dressage whip: Normal conditions (A), and with my left rein open, allowing me, with the flick of the wrist, to make contact with the horse and not hit my leg (B).

2 This is a two-step process, first open the rein and then rotate your wrist. With practice it can become seamless.

Most times this will bring out a buck, so be ready. If he does buck, I would go to your whip again and repeat until the bucking stops. You may end up at a full gallop around the arena. But, I can assure you, you'll stamp out this problem within a few days if you stick with it.

6 You are also going to make sure that when you transition down to trot, it is *your* idea—alone. There should be none of this "mutual agreement to trot," and it certainly can't be *his* idea! Should he break into the trot before you ask, get back as quickly as you can into the canter. It does you no good when he breaks from the canter and you then walk to think about it for a minute before asking for the canter again. Your horse just won! He took a break to relish his victory and will now be back ready to fight again. Make sure you use every possible training opportunity.

Solution B

Another trick to increase your success rate is to use lateral movements as tools to require your horse to remain in front of your leg. In the same way as you expect your horse to move forward off your leg, he must be just as responsive to moving sideways off your leg. This not only gets him tuned into you, but also forces him to engage his hind end. And this, in the end, is your main goal.

Solution C

Now, at this point, you have the walk, trot, and canter all set. Let's move on to jumping. The same basic principle applies. Make sure you have an active trot or canter before approaching your jump. Jump it and canter away with conviction. It's your responsibility to convince the horse that he has one option, that is, to leave the fence with the same energy level and in the same balance that he had when he arrived at it. If this is not the case, you have a problem on your hands. Fix it! If you are not comfortable getting after your horse over a jump, then go back a step with just a rail on the ground. Again, make sure you come out on top in more ways than one.

▶ **Cause Four:** *The Cold-Backed Bucker*

This is one of the few problems that you cannot address directly because it doesn't have a behavioral root cause. Horses that buck from this are nearly impossible to stop, though the behavior will tend to diminish with time. You need to be patient!

I don't get bucked off often, but nearly every time it's happened on a horse that is cold-backed. It is truly a pain—or discomfort—issue. You are best served by proceeding slowly and methodically so the horse is completely confident you are not going to hurt him.

This third type of bucking is something I'd be much more careful about regardless of how good you are at sticking on bucking horses. Cold-backed horses were briefly covered in chapter 3 (p. 31). I want to reiterate here that you should make sure you are aware of clues your horse is giving you when working around him.

The first time you tack up a horse pay attention to how sensitive he is when you tighten the girth. Some are very sensitive, so with these horses, proceed with caution.

Solution A

If the horse seems worried or jumpy as you start to tighten the girth, leave it snug but not tight, and take him for a short walk. Walking him in between tightening the girth in stages allows him to become more accustomed to the girth's pressure and the feeling of the saddle moving on his back. He will become more comfortable and you can then tighten the girth the rest of the way.

tip *Keep in mind a horse that was sensitive to being tacked up might also be extra sensitive when the weight of a rider is applied. When you get on a cold-backed horse, be very careful and "soft" during the first few minutes of riding him. Once he is moving around, walking, trotting and cantering, you're generally in good shape and shouldn't have to worry.*

Solution B

When you ride an unfamiliar horse for the first time, regardless of what his owner has told you, proceed with caution. It's very possible that he may begin bucking just as you mount.

When mounting for the first time, I strongly recommend placing your left foot in the stirrup putting all of your weight in it and not swinging your leg right over to the far side. Lean over the horse instead so if he bolts or tries to take off bucking, you'll be able to dismount without injury (see fig. 4.2 B, p. 42).

Once you feel confident enough to swing your leg over, I make a fuss over the horse. Pet him on both sides of his neck, though use caution when patting him behind the saddle. The most sensitive horses can be set off by the smallest trigger.

Solution C

Once you've successfully mounted your cold-backed horse (or, for that matter, one just being started), he may feel as if he's "frozen," or of more concern, completely relaxed. Be very careful as you ask him to walk forward. You might get a massive bucking spree rather than the relaxed walk you were hoping to achieve.

Ask him to move off into the walk with just a very gentle leg pressure. If he is going to buck, now is the time. Be ready by sitting back with your reins short. When you put your leg on and he humps his back, take your leg off quickly! And, this is not the time to use your whip.

Give him a moment; you should feel his back relax again. This time instead of trying to get him to move directly forward, open your rein and try to get him to move sideways. Some will move off normally. If not then slowly and quietly try to get him moving in a small circle. The moment he steps sideways you should again be able to move forward. Just take your time. Your warm up may take a few more minutes, but once going, you shouldn't have any trouble.

Solution D

The most difficult horses will take one or two steps sideways and again hump their back. You feel as if you are sitting on a huge roach! Once more, I'll stop and stand there until I feel his back relax. Just keep slowly asking him to turn and eventually you'll be able to make a small circle and then go forward, progressively increasing the diameter until you feel comfortable continuing on your ride.

If he does happen to try to buck, as quickly as possible, yank his head up. I don't use a lot of leg or the whip in this case. You need to provide a comfortable situation for the cold-backed horse, not one of harsh consequences. Again, it's not his choice, but for whatever reason, he is just not comfortable.

Solution E

Stay aware of your surroundings. Be extra particular about the footing or ground where you are mounting. Personally, I take one of these horses into the ring: If I'm going to hit the dirt I don't want to do it on a stone or asphalt driveway, just somewhere with a soft landing. Watch out for dogs and children. This type of horse can be set off by something popping out from behind a trailer or a building.

It might sound strange, but I also pay attention to how level the ground is. I had a horse that was particularly cold-backed. We had to tighten the girth one hole at a time— walking him in between—until the saddle was secure enough to mount. This particular venue was built on a hill. Once on his back, I had to walk 50 feet or so before heading up a slight hill toward the warm-up arenas. The moment we stepped up the grade he immediately began bucking. I had to retreat to the level surface and walk around it for a few minutes before I was able to ride up the hill without him bucking.

A Learning Experience

Often, talent and bucking go hand in hand. One of the most talented horses I've had the pleasure of competing has planted me on the ground more times than I can count. He has since gone on to win a number of National Championships and countless events and dressage shows.

When first starting him, things went very smoothly for the first few weeks. We got to the point of riding around alone: walk, trot and a little bit of canter. After finishing one day's ride, I let him hang out in the middle of the ring while I helped a student. A few minutes later, I asked him to move forward to walk back to the barn. Without warning, I was struggling to maintain my balance and remain on top as he bucked around the indoor! With the wall quickly approaching—and its ominous steel pillars—I was dreading my "dismount." As he cut left, I started to fall to the right; knowing the end was near, I did my best to get my upper body off to the left and away from the wall.

While making an unplanned dismount was not ideal, I was very happy to have been able to at least avoid the pillars. I was much more careful with him after this, though unfortunately, I've hit the dirt a number of times since. This was odd really, seeing that he didn't exhibit many signs early on that he could be a bit cold-backed. It's not an issue when in work, but following a day off or more, I'm very careful for the first few minutes.

Bolting

What Happens

In a bolt, your horse is reacting to a trigger, often from behind him, that causes a sharp burst of acceleration from your present gait to a full gallop. Due to his innate instinctual habits, your horse will first flee from a threat and assess it later.

Bolting horses, in most cases, are looking to escape a perceived threat. Horses instinctually are fight-or-flight creatures. You can be proud of your bolter—he would be considered a superior being if only he lived in the wild. Although he may think that everything is out to get him, your job is to convince him that this isn't the case.

Very much like rearing, your horse may be using bolting to intimidate you (fig. II.6). On occasion, just like rearing, it may be caused by fear, but when it happens often, he's using the behavior to train you! Once he's asked to do

II.6 Simon, formally called Shining North Star, has just been startled and is beginning to bolt. Seeing that there is a fence on the left, I'm just beginning to open my right rein to unlock his neck and prevent him from grabbing the bit to bolt farther.

something he doesn't feel like doing, he bolts. In order not to set off a bolt, the rider soon becomes less and less demanding of him, and the horse gets his way.

▶ Cause One

In nearly all cases of bolting, there is an external trigger (or excuse) that "sets him off." It might be something as seemingly innocuous as a leaf blowing in the wind, a loud noise, or other horses spooking. The reasons are endless.

II.7 My right hand is braced on the horse's neck and I'm pulling with my left.

Solution A

The mechanics of the fix are really quite simple. The moment your horse starts to bolt, *turn* him. Turning can be difficult at times, so keep in mind the technique you were taught the first day you got on your pony: The pulley rein is very effective!

Simply pull on one rein as hard as you can manage because your horse will not be able to run quickly on a small circle (fig. II.7). As you pull he will begin to turn, and as the radius diminishes, he will slow down. The moment you have him on a circle, you will be back to working conditions soon.

You will have limited-to-no success stopping a bolter by pulling directly backward. Your horse's neck is more than 10 times bigger and stronger than your arms. If he really wants to take you for a ride, he's more than capable.

Solution B

To stop him more quickly, when your horse consistently bolts you may want to try a stronger bit to make an impression on him that it's not such a good idea. As always, I'm hesitant to go to a harsher bit, but if the running away is happening often, or you can't stop him when he does bolt, it is probably the safer option.

tip *Regardless of how fast he is going or what he's approaching, it's not worth bailing out! I haven't met one person who has fallen off intentionally with a positive outcome. Riders generally end up hurt, with their horse running loose. Or, they return with a lot of unnecessary wear and tear at best. You don't want to think about a worst-case scenario—a loose horse galloping at full speed—so do your best to stay on where at least you'll have some control.*

▶ Cause Two

In extreme cases, horses can bolt from what they perceive as "absolute confinement" from the rider. This is a rare occurrence, but if you happen to be working with a horse that has had a very "questionable" past, you should be wary. Horses that have been abused can, at times, "snap" and bolt.

Solution

You must be very careful and compassionate with this type of horse. Often, the rider will apply an aid, the horse will initially seem not to react, then he'll "blow up" and bolt. You are very likely to experience this type of reaction after a horse "freezes." But regardless of his initial behavior, your best bet is to try to turn him. Adding leg will most likely make the problem worse. Once frozen you're looking to get his feet moving. Usually, the moment you get a circle started with an opening rein, the horse will snap back into "normal" mode.

tip *I can't reiterate enough that you must exercise caution and care in all these cases of possible abuse in the horse's history. Getting after your horse does not work. It just makes the problem worse!*

Spooking

What Happens

Just like the bolter, the "spooker" has usually been scared by something and is reacting by spinning away because he perceives the trigger as a threat. Some horses are afraid of one particular object, while others don't like specific colors or going from light to dark. Still others seem to be frightened of everything including their own shadow. In all cases, your horse first locks the brakes up; soon after he will drop one shoulder and spin in that direction, allowing a quick exit stage left!

As with a number of the problems discussed so far, when you pay close enough attention you should be able to pick up spooking "patterns." Although the horse does not always stick to the script, your job is to anticipate. You need to quickly be able to get into a defensive riding position and react (figs. II.8 A–I). Without this position, you're sunk!

II.8 A–I The initial spook will take you by surprise. If you keep your center of gravity above the horse's and your shoulders back, you should remain in the tack (A–F). I begin to be able to open my right rein and establish a bend and direction (G). He begins to turn right (H). Now I will head back to whatever scared him in order to show him that it was not such a big deal (I)!

Horses that exhibit this behavior, in general, have very little self-confidence. They will spin and try to leave the area because they don't have a strong leader. They will continue to spook for as long as they think that you are putting them in a dangerous situation. It's your job to instill the confidence they need that allows them to grow.

▶ **Cause One**

In most cases, a horse spooks at a particular object, or at something or someone that pops up quickly. The prime example is the dog that runs out from the woods or from behind the barn: Your horse will drop his shoulder or stop and spin to "get out of town." Spooking is a tricky behavior to anticipate, and unfortunately, it happens without advanced warning. You can only hope that you can weather the initial storm, then deal with the consequences.

Solution A

The moment you feel the spook begin you need to figure out which direction your horse is looking to go. Let's say he starts to turn left:

1 As quickly as you can manage, open your right rein and put on as much left leg as you can. Your goal is to counteract any movement by your horse.

2 It may take a few strides to start to get him back on track. Once you've got him under control, make a point to yield him off his left leg since that was the one he used to evade.

3 With luck a friend is around to catch the dog and take him back behind the shed and set your horse up for the same occurrence. To cure this type of problem, you need to be able to put your horse in the same situation. Without repetition your chances of solving the problem are slim.

4 If you can orchestrate it, have your friend hold the dog out of view. You are going to ask for the dog to be let go on your command. But, before you give the okay to release the dog, start to leg-yield your horse to the right to an extreme extent: Your goal is to intentionally "pop" the horse's right shoulder with an opening right rein and over-bend his body to the left. This positioning gives you the best odds of preventing the left spook and spin.

5 Repeat this process until you don't lose control. You are never going to eliminate a "startle" reaction from a horse, but with training and exposure, you can limit the time this sort of incident negatively affects your ride.

Solution B

With a horse like this, your goal is to get him out of his comfort zone as often as possible. It can be something as easy as changing his surroundings and moving jumps around in the ring each day, to a daily trail ride through the woods. Every time you are in a new environment, make sure your riding position is secure and ready for anything. This is not the horse you need to get ahead of with your upper body—when you do, you'll soon find yourself heading for the ground!

Solution C

If you happen to be unlucky enough to have a horse that is afraid of anything and everything, I have bad news for you. When dealing with a horse like this your best bet is to keep exposing him to new items and scenarios at every opportunity: You want to make him immune to the normal type of distractions seen in competition or on the trail. These might include a cooler lying over a fence, a tractor, or an umbrella in the ring. Let your creativity run wild—the crazier, the better! But at the back of your mind, remember that some horses, unfortunately, never recover from such an affliction.

▶ **Cause Two**

The competitive environment causes some horses to have extreme show nerves or show spookiness.

Solution A

Your working plan for the spooky horse in competition is the polar opposite from your training at home. In this case you do your best to **avoid** any potential distraction—in your warm up and in the ring. Your goal is to limit his exposure to anything that might trigger the explosive response. This habit, without a doubt, can be improved, but it is not going to be eliminated anytime soon. So, to get ready, implement Solution C on p. 115, then in warm-up for the competition, do your very best to avoid distractions.

The upside of the spooky horse is that he is often more energetic and generally a better jumper. You can use his spooky nature to your advantage: Lines and approaches when jumping can be more aggressive. Knowing he is going to be super careful, go for the win! Some of the best jumpers I've competed are also the spookiest horses I've ridden.

Barn Sour/Nappy/Drops the Shoulder

What Happens

Horses are inherently lazy creatures—some with a better work ethic than others. Unfortunately, the "nappy" horse was not born with one! He will spin or plant his feet so that he doesn't have to work. If the rider does not succeed in convincing him that he must go, there is no good reason he will change this habit.

Taking a look again at the horse's evolution, barn-sour or nappy horses are probably closer to their wild relatives than most domestic horses. It's a fact of life that horses are, by nature, herd animals. Of course, we don't generally like them to exhibit these instinctive behaviors when we are out riding.

A horse is a creature of habit. When he is reluctant to leave where he is—or, in this case, the opposite, he wants to leave where you've taken him—your job is to identify what the "magnet" is that's drawing him and its direction. At home this might be the barn or the field where his pals are turned out. At a show, it can be where the trailer is parked or the warm-up arena.

Once you have identified the attraction, make sure that regardless of what he "throws at you," you don't allow him to get back to where he wants to go. You must finish with the upper hand, otherwise you've got a very long road ahead.

▶ Cause One

Imagine you're looking to leave the barn and head down a lane to your ring. Since leaving the barn, your horse has been walking toward the ring, but very reluctantly. You get 100 meters down the path, and very quickly he drops his right shoulder, grabs the left rein and begins to bolt back to the barn.

Solution A

When your horse drops his right shoulder and spins right, never mind how long it takes—you must turn him *left* to get back to where you came from. All too often, you see a horse run to the right, and because it's easier to turn right, the rider takes the right rein, and turns him in a complete circle. When this happens (that is, the rider turns the horse in the direction he has spun), the rider has, in effect, made the horse think he's just come away victorious.

1 Obviously, you must first stop the horse from bolting—this is paramount. If a pulley rein is necessary, use it, but keep in mind, seeing that he turned right, your goal is to turn him left to return to the path.

2 As I just mentioned, if you turn *right,* he's won, and he'll continue to exploit your weakness indefinitely. You'll end up getting farther away from the arena with every attempt; each time he'll use the same trick of turning right. Be sure not to fall into his trap.

3 In this case use your left rein as the pulley rein. Once you have him stopped, turn him back to the path. Ultimately, you have to get after him with your leg and whip, but you do have some other considerations.

4 If you are not careful you can cause the horse to rear, so make sure not to pull directly back on the left rein. Using an opening rein is key to keeping his front feet on the ground.

5 A horse that drops his shoulder is quite smart, and usually athletic, too. Not unlike when riding in the arena, you have to make sure you "turn" his shoulders. You cannot use a driving aid effectively until his body is pointed in the direction you want to go. When his head is pointed down the lane to the ring, but his shoulder is to the right and his body 45 degrees to the path, the more leg you apply, the more crooked he'll become. So your action requires precise timing.

Turn him back to the lane and once his withers are in line with this path, add as much leg and whip as you can muster. Some horses respond well to a tap of the whip on the shoulder (right side, in this example) to help get them pointed in the correct direction again.

6 When he moves on forward, you can relax your leg. But, a few seconds later a horse with this habit will quickly become less responsive to your leg so keep "checking in" by adding light leg pressure. He should be nearly jumping forward with its application. If he doesn't, add that same light leg again and simultaneously use your whip for reinforcement. At this point, you should have your horse marching toward the arena.

Solution B

The next step is *prevention*. Seeing that the horse likes to drop his right shoulder, integrate lateral-suppling exercises throughout your ride each day, concentrating on his response to your right leg. When you anticipate that he might become nappy, or he begins to shut down, immediately try to over-bend him to the right, with his left shoulder slightly popping out. This positioning will make it much harder for him to drop the right shoulder.

Perhaps even more importantly, stay very strict. He must stay responsive to your leg. From the moment you get on, when you add light leg pressure, his response should be prompt and active. Imagine your horse has cruise control installed: You tell him the gait, energy level, tempo and balance you want and he maintains them all until you tell him otherwise. And, no crawling, or plodding along—he doesn't need to warm up to walk actively forward. Even when cooling him out on a long rein, walk with a purpose!

In the previous problem (spooking), I talked about a horse that drops the shoulder and spins (p. 112). This is one of many expressions of displeasure your horse can choose to demonstrate; these can also include rearing, bucking, or simply stopping. In order to prevent all these behaviors, you have to identify the behavior's trigger and prevent the horse from encountering the conditions that allow the trigger to be activated.

Unclear Transition with Unexpected Results

What Happens

You ask your horse to move on from walk to trot. Instead of trotting he breaks into a very slow canter. The moment you attempt to slow him down he again walks. You have a very smart and slightly lazy horse that has figured out that if he canters instead of trotting, you will bring him back to the walk. He repeats this indefinitely and never actually has to trot—or work—for that matter. There are a few others who may take it one step further with a buck or kick out to your leg when you ask for the trot. The solutions remain the same.

▶ Cause One

Your horse is green and has misunderstood what is being asked.

Solution

Start off at the walk; ask him into the trot. When instead of trotting, the horse breaks into the canter, you have to realize that by cantering after being asked to trot, he's actually just doing more than you asked. Congratulations, you have an overachiever! So allow him to canter a few strides, ask him to come back to a trot, repeat the walk-to-trot transition with more subtle aids, and the trot should be no problem.

▶ Cause Two

You have an intelligent horse that has figured out a way to live a lazy existence.

Solution A

Note: This solution is intended for the lazier type and should not be used for a hot horse—one recently off the track, for example.

You ask for a trot and your horse breaks into a very slow, short-strided canter. Most riders bring the horse back to the walk in an attempt to ask for the transition again. Unfortunately, the same scenario develops every time. In this case, ask the horse to trot, and when he goes into the tiny canter, gallop him forward. Don't just canter a little faster, *make it count*. You need to make the horse realize that by cantering while being asked for a trot, he's going to have to work even harder. Once you gallop forward at least 15 strides, ask him down to a trot. If he again goes into the tiny canter, then gallop forward again. Repeat this process until you're back trotting.

Solution B

As you prepare to ask for the trot, begin a leg-yield away from your inside leg. By moving laterally you require your horse to step under with his inside hind leg. (As he steps sideways, he must also step more forward, otherwise he'll step on himself.) The moment he steps forward, he will be more likely to trot. Once in the trot, continue the leg-yield for a few steps. Your goal is to again make sure the trot is forward and active.

Tracking Up

How do you know if a trot is active enough? Have a ground person in the ring with you. Ask her to tell you when and if the horse is, at least, tracking up. When I say "tracking up" I mean the hind foot should land in the footprint of the front foot. Better yet is when you can get your horse to "over-track," which means the hind footprint lands in front of the front footprint. This is true of a good walk and trot. Most people are too complacent and happy with an underpowered gait, but it leads to an unsteady contact and connection, resulting in many problems down the road. There are a few horses that do not naturally have the stride to track up at the trot; in these cases, your goal is to get them as close as you can.

Solution C

When you ask your horse to move into the trot he may bolt or run uncontrollably forward. If you feel completely out of control and cannot slow him down using normal means, then employ a pulley rein. Many of us were taught this technique as a child in Pony Club. It was essential then with a bratty pony, but it still comes in handy today!

Take hold of the inside rein, placing your other hand on his neck, and pull as hard as you can. A horse will not be able to continue to bolt as the circle diameter becomes smaller. Don't worry about looking pretty, just get the job done. Your safety is much more important than your appearance. Once back at a walk, go onto a small circle, 8 meters or so. From here, practice spiraling in and out to make sure that you have control and that your horse is listening and willingly yielding from your leg pressure. Once established, begin to spiral in as you ask him to trot. If he starts to bolt, continue to spiral in and you'll soon return to a reasonable pace. Continue to repeat until you can maintain an acceptable trot, at which point you can start to spiral out, eventually making it to the perimeter of the arena.

A Learning Experience

Many times the most talented horses are the quirkiest ones you'll ever deal with. One of the best horses I've ever had the opportunity to ride was just that quirky! His name is Running Order; he started with us never having evented and was sold following his first CCI**** at Rolex Kentucky. There is a more detailed story about him later on (see p. 204), but as for being barn sour, he was one of the worst.

Luckily for me, that's the only reason I was given the ride. He was incredibly smart, he was slightly scared of everything, and he also found it amusing to "pull your chain." He was one of the few horses that generally behaved very well, but if someone new was riding him, or he saw an opportunity when you weren't paying attention, he'd drop his shoulder and bolt in the opposite direction—back to the barn.

Cross-country schooling, especially the first few times of the year, was always a challenge. Even after competing at the Advanced Level, it would take me five minutes to get him over a one-foot high log or brush jump! How did I deal with it? Well, I'll be honest, he tested me on a daily basis. He would keep me on my toes: At even at the slightest blip, hesitation, or cocked ear, I'd respond as if he'd just spun and bolted. This way it never escalated to that point. The only catch seemed to occur when we returned from a trip out of town; he would revert very quickly back to his old habits, so often, the first day back included a gallop down the driveway! From then on, we were good to go until the next trip away.

The Stubborn "Freeze"

What Happens
Very much like the barn-sour horse (see p. 116), the stubborn freeze will get your horse out of work. He is a little more of a passive-aggressive type, but the story is the same. If you can't convince him to get to work, why should he?

The *stubborn freeze* is a whole different ball game (fig. 11.9). You're most likely sitting on a calm, laid-back calculating beast! When he smells "blood in the water," he's going to put his mental game into high gear and go for the kill. Most times, the stubborn freeze occurs on a hack, or when heading in a direction the horse has decided he is not inclined to continue on. (Be careful not to

11.9 Horses will often freeze in a very alert pose so be cautious— and tactful!

diagnose this condition with a nervous horse that is, instead, simply paralyzed by fear—see p. 124.)

Just as with the "nappy" horse, you have to bring the fear of God into his mind. You must convince him you're crazier than he is, and you'll win at all cost! I hope you have your crop handy, seeing that it's going to get some use.

▶ **Cause One**

Ultimately, you have a lazy, stubborn horse that thinks he's quite smart. You might be leaving the barn heading down to the ring or just out on the trail. But wherever you are, your horse just plants his feet and decides he'd rather stop and stand than proceed.

Solution

The very first time this occurs you'll have to react quickly. It's best if I discuss prevention first, though. This horse is obviously "behind your leg," which means he's not being responsive enough to your applied aid. As it turns out, the problem seldom raises its ugly head when you are in the ring, so you discover it when you go outside. It's the same with the lazy horses I discussed earlier in this section. So again, add a light leg pressure and when you don't get a prompt active response, ask again and back up your leg with a swift, firm strike of your crop.

▶ **Cause Two**

Let's take the following situation to its conclusion. You are riding your horse in the arena, and he's just starting medium trot and canter. All is going very well. He's responsive in his upward and downward transitions. You decide as a reward that you'll take him for a little walk on the trail.

You get a few minutes away from the barn and as you approach a clearing entering a field, the dreaded freeze happens. You can't get him to go any farther. He might feel as if he is thinking of rearing or spinning but those are not his weapons of choice. He's drawn a line in the sand and will not go forward anymore.

Solution

Even on a walk aimed at being a relaxing alternative to working in the ring, you must remain vigilant. Every now and then check in with your horse. Add a light amount of leg. If you don't get the desired response, follow the aid with a prompt and firm strike of your crop! If this does not work, instantly do it again. Continue this process, increasing the pressure until your horse marches forward.

Nervous and Anxious

What Happens

Most anxious horses don't have a mean bone in their body; they are just hypersensitive to their environment and to what is being asked of them. They can't help getting nervous and, for them to progress, you must find a way to provide comfort.

Riding a nervous horse can be a most frustrating experience, but it is paramount that any negative emotions on your part never play a role in your solution. The anxiety that a horse displays can have infinite root causes, and your goal is to investigate and determine which it is that sets him off, and throughout the process, help him to gain confidence. Once the horse is confident, his anxiety will subside. Compassion is your weapon of choice in this matter.

As with most behavioral issues I like to first rule out physical problems that may be contributing. Often a nervous horse is that way because he is affected by ulcers, which can prove to have a debilitating effect on your horse's health and performance. You might be very surprised how treating him will give you a drastic improvement in his behavior. So if you have an anxious horse, have a GI scope inspection done by your local veterinarian to check for ulcers. They are not complicated to treat today.

Most nervous horses do better with plenty of turnout and higher percentage of roughage in their diet. You should also do your best to avoid feeds that are high in simple carbohydrates. As with people, food that can be converted into sugar makes horses more nervous and excitable.

▶ Cause One

Anxiety is frequently caused by a lack of confidence. What are the signs that your horse is a nervous one? Symptoms range from the subtle to the dramatic: Rapid chewing of the bit; excessive sweating; quivering; opening and closing the mouth repeatedly; teeth being ground all the way down; and never completely relaxing the body are just a few. This leaves your horse with a very tight core, which makes lateral exercises difficult.

Also be aware there are horses that internalize their emotions, though their problems are not always obvious to the casual observer. I've encountered a few horses that outwardly seemed quite confident, but in actuality, were very anxious and always wanting to please—as I discovered later. If your horse is a jumper and you've had trouble with him being nappy at the in-gate or stopping at jumps, he may have been overfaced or he's lacking in confidence (see pp. 160 and 128).

Solution A

Contrary to intuition, a hot horse does better—and is more relaxed—with the more leg you use. If you haven't read about the research that Temple Grandin pioneered, it would be of value to do so. She is an autistic researcher who has developed compression blankets for dogs affected by thunder storms, as well as humane slaughter houses for the commercial meat industry, among many other inventions and process improvements for livestock and people. She discovered (and uses it on herself) that animals become more relaxed with a constant pressure around their body. She uses foam padded panels to compress the livestock. Your legs can have a similar effect so imagine that they are going to "hug" your horse—not as a driving aid all the time, but as an always present constant.

All too often, you see "hyper" or "hot" horses with their riders sitting in a chair-seat position with their legs completely off their horse and, coincidentally, the horse is distraught and leaping around like a monkey. These riders would be so much better off wrapping their legs around the horse and giving him a job to do to make him concentrate! Along with leg pressure, make sure you always have contact with your horse's mouth. I am constantly amazed how often I see people riding with inconsistent rein pressure, thus with no contact. The whole idea behind training is to gain the horse's trust; there will be no incentive for him to stretch into the contact if he's not convinced (and trusts) that it will be there at every moment. He's obviously worried about his surroundings or what's being asked of him, so you need to be there for him!

Solution B

Horses are happiest and most relaxed when they are confident they can perform what is being asked, and also when they are appropriately challenged in order to avoid boredom. Try to imagine that your horse's brain is in a constant state of overdrive and that you need to make sure all of that "processing power" is going to something productive. The less you ask of him, the fewer constructive ideas his brain will work to process.

Lateral work is your friend. Not only are you asking your horse to figure out what is being asked, but the lateral work forces him to start to take longer strides, and ultimately, to physically "use" his topline and relax. In a leg-yield, for instance, when the horse is asked to move sideways, he must step forward and sideways to avoid stepping on himself with his inside hind leg. As he steps forward and under, he's becoming more engaged and can then more effectively use his hind end for propulsion.

▶ Cause Two

A nervous horse can "freeze"—a situation where he completely locks up his body and refuses to move. This feeling makes me just about as nervous as I ever am on a horse. If it doesn't make you a little anxious, it should! When your horse encounters something he's scared of, or is just so anxious that he doesn't feel he can proceed, he may freeze. It is very much like sitting on a time bomb waiting to explode, the trouble being that when he *does* explode, you have no idea which direction he'll be heading. Sometimes this freeze can also be matched with shaking or just an overall jittery feeling. Often you can feel his heart beating between your legs. Make sure not to confuse stubborn stopping (a deliberate refusal to go forward) with that of nervous behavior. The following solution should be applied *only* for a problem with its roots in anxiety.

Solution A

At this "time-bomb" moment, the worst thing you can do is add a "driving" force: leg or whip. Your best bet is to try to turn out of the situation. Use an opening inside rein—it really doesn't matter in which direction. Softly open the rein, and starting with an extremely light pressure, slowly increase the rein contact in order to turn until he snaps out of it.

If you feel you may be unseated, use your outside hand to grab hold of the saddle, breastplate, neck strap or saddle strap. Normally, the moment he moves, the action will be quick but short-lived. You'll almost feel as if he's jumped in the direction of the open rein. Fortunately, most horses jig or walk out of it, though some might bolt.

Breeds of Horses with Nervous Tendencies

In general there are two main types of horses that fall into the "Nervous and Anxious" category. Many people would guess that nervous traits are only found in Thoroughbreds, but what about the draft crosses? I can't tell you how many horses I've been sent that were purchased by people just starting their riding career looking for a level-headed, quiet partner. They have gone to an auction to buy a Premarin (PMU) rescue foal—usually a draft cross with very little handling—or another horse of questionable background thinking they can "learn together." This is a horrible idea! There are many "quirky" draft horses out there. These horses, when spooked, are happy to just bolt over you if they perceive their life is in danger. Unfortunately, it's not much better once you're on their back. Again they will blindly run when spooked, meaning you are just a fly on their back hanging on for the ride. Like a bulldozer, they'll run through anything, and I mean *anything,* in their way. Sometimes there are very hazardous results.

Thoroughbreds, on the other hand, have self-preservation on their side, as well as being exceptionally athletic. Many of them were also brought up in a "circus" environment on the track, meaning that they have been handled by 100-plus people. This generally translates into good manners on the ground and a healthy respect for your personal space.

⁕ tip *When you have a horse that freezes, be very careful that you're not using too much hand in your riding. Most horses don't freeze on a whim: They often feel confined as if there is no way out.*

As a rule of thumb, make sure you always have a ratio of two times as much leg as hand, and make absolutely sure when you add leg that you allow your horse to move forward away from it. He needs to know that he is always able to move forward and is not confined.

Solution B

If he does bolt, look to change his direction and initiate a turn, then establish bend and slow him down with the outside rein (see Bolting, p. 110). Try to stop him in the slowest, kindest way possible. Yanking on the rein or trying to stop him abruptly will oftentimes exacerbate your problem at this point. Although this can be frustrating, do your best to continue to be as soft and caring as possible.

▶ Cause Three

When you have a horse that appears nervous but often finds excuses not to work or can be distracted easily, you very well might be making him just plain bored!

Solution

Frequently, nervous horses are very smart. With their brain in a constant state of overdrive, they can often learn at a faster rate. You have to remember when you are training a horse like this that he is also extremely sensitive—an overachiever that is hypersensitive to correction. While a moderate amount of leg might be enough to get an average horse's attention when he does something wrong, with a nervous horse, you may well get the same response from a very light leg. All training concepts are the same; however, imagine you're working with the fine adjustment dial rather than the coarse one.

The Horse That Lacks Confidence

What Happens

Just like the nervous type, the horse that lacks confidence is looking for your support. He may show it in slightly different ways, but he is looking for a sympathetic but strong leader he can rely on.

While he may have survived in the wild, this horse doesn't do so well in the domestic horse world. Your job is to instill confidence in him. In most cases, a horse that lacks confidence has not been shown the way forward. He needs you to lead him in the correct direction! In the following examples, let's assume the horse is one who wouldn't hurt a fly—he is a genuine type who seldom questions you.

▶ **Cause One**

Whether you are starting this horse out for the first time, retraining him after his career on the track, or performing a different discipline, he doesn't enjoy leaving his friends. He gets nervous, anxious and, very often, is quite spooky. In this example, we have a horse that, when leaving the barn, draws a "line in the sand" that he will not cross. It might be at the edge of the property, a clearing, or just an arbitrary point.

Solution

The first thing I do is take a confident rider on an educated horse along with you. We start all the "babies" on the trail or on hacks with friends. There is no better way to demonstrate to your horse what is expected of him than to have another horse show him the way. Usually the "chicken" horse doesn't stay one forever; it might be his tendency but not a lifelong affliction.

Exercise

1 With your friend leading you down the path toward the clearing, do a few quick tests, making sure that there is a prompt response to your leg. I add a light leg, and if he doesn't jump forward, I back up my leg up with the whip. Depending on the horse, I use enough whip to make a point so that he jumps forward, but not so much that he bolts. The idea is not to terrify him, just to make sure that when you approach his stopping point, you have a tool to work with.

2 I also make sure he is not hanging on to either rein significantly more than the other. When he is heavy, it gives him a very easy option to dislodge you and allow him to "drop the anchor." If he is heavy on one side versus the other, you can use some exercises you learned in the ring to get you out of trouble here as well (see Contact Issues, p. 65).

3 Now that your horse is responsive and marching forward, continue to follow your friend along the trail and check frequently to make sure he is just as responsive to your leg as he was a minute ago. It's amazing how quickly he can shut down. The closer you get to the line in the sand the more aggressive your corrections should be: It's acceptable for the horse to be caught "sleeping" and need a reminder the first time around, but after repeated reminders about listening to your leg, the consequences should become more dramatic.

4 That said, as you approach the stopping point keep your friend in front, and your horse actively behind. If your horse starts to stall go right back to your leg—and whip, if necessary. Ask your friend to keep walking, horses are herd bound and your horse is probably more so than the average. I would bet that nine times out of ten your horse will follow along without question.

5 When he does follow along okay, turn around so you can reapproach the same spot—this time, with you in the lead. If your horse stops, you must become aggressive with your leg and whip, while asking your friend to walk by you. Repeat this process until you can walk over the line without adding any extra leg at all, with your friend behind you.

The Bully

What Happens
Just like a bully in school, the horse will use fear tactics to intimidate you in order to get his way.

Now, instead of a "chicken" you're working with a "pig." The chicken approaches the "line in the sand" with his ears pricked forward and actively investigates the problem in front of him. He may end up jumping backward quickly, but just as fast he'll jump forward in recognition that you're asking him to go forward. He is just trying to figure out what the line is all about. The pig approaches the same line, and couldn't care less about what you'd like to do. He is out for his own goals, certainly not yours!

I would rather fix this problem on my own without another horse and rider along. The friend can be used in the most extreme cases only. The reason I don't want anybody is because this type of horse does not care if his friend is in front, behind, or on top of him. His reluctance is not rooted in fear or misunderstanding—he simply doesn't feel the need to go farther. Unlike the chicken, this horse does not care to learn what you're trying to teach him. Many times the "bullies" are anything but lacking in confidence. When dealing with a horse like this try to act like a drill sergeant in basic training. Frankly, he could do with getting knocked down a few pegs!

▶ **Cause One**

Using the same example of a line in the sand, your horse just stops dead, sending a clear message that he's not going any farther. He is stubborn and "drops anchor."

Solution A

Have your whip out and ready. I usually ride in a jumping saddle because a horse like this might be unpredictable when you get after him. Your job is to convince him that you're the crazier one in the relationship. He has to listen to you—or else!

Start off down the path using the same starting point, and same procedure as with the chicken (see p. 129). Ask him to move on, and if he doesn't jump forward use your whip as reinforcement. As you approach the "line in the sand," you're going to have to muster up all of your strength. He's going to do his best to shut down just a few feet before the line. I have my reins bridged and ready in my left hand with my whip in my right at the ready (see p. 104). The moment he tries to shut down, go right to the leg and whip simultaneously, and repeat it as quickly as possible until you're past the spot in question. Don't worry about being too harsh, seeing that the moment he *does* go forward, you're going to instantly turn into the kindest, softest rider you can imagine, petting him all the way home. Don't hold a grudge, just make sure your point is clear: You don't take no for an answer!

Solution B

In the very worst cases, if the horse still has the upper hand or you feel in danger, it's time to call in reinforcement. This can come in many ways: I first bring a friend for support and use the same strategy I mentioned with the not so confident horse, getting a lead when needed (see p. 129). If you still have no luck, it may be worth looking to find a local professional who can assist you further—one who is familiar with dealing with problems like this.

Jumping Problems

General Jumping Philosophy

First off, when you approach a fence, your horse must have no option other than to figure out how to get over safely to the other side. Your responsibility is to make sure that the jump is safe. You must never take a chance on this because it's vitally important the horse absolutely believes he is capable of safely jumping what's in front of him. The moment you ask him to go over something with a questionable landing or poor construction and, as a result, you happen to have a "bad" jump or landing, your horse will begin to question whether he should listen to you next time you ask him to jump something new or different. This said, I don't blame him. He should not trust you!

Most riders are committed to jump a fence, but sometimes a new, maybe intimidating, jump can give you concern. But, you must not waver in your desire to jump the jump: A horse's intuition about this sort of thing is usually spot on. If he detects reservation on your part, you may as well not try the fence at all than attempt it half-heartedly.

The jump you are presenting should be within your horse's scope and at an appropriate level for him. This is essential to building confidence. When in doubt, come back another day to jump a bigger or more complicated fence.

It's always better to come out of your jump school with your horse feeling like a rock star rather than a kid who has just been betrayed (and then scolded!) by his mother—or worse yet, injured.

With all that said, you must have enough *energy*, *pace*, *direction*, and *balance:*

• *Energy:* The energy level should always be quite high: This does not mean frantic, but actually quite relaxed. For those who can drive a car with a manual transmission, imagine downshifting before you attempt to jump: You want to have high rpms but a relatively slow ground speed. This is a difficult concept, but like everything in life, it will come in time. It's always helpful to have educated eyes on the ground to confirm your feel. Ultimately, you want power to spare: In case you get into a sticky situation, you'll have plenty of opportunity to get out unscathed.

• *Pace:* The appropriate pace to jump a fence can vary drastically with its type, the conditions, location, and terrain. It also varies according to the width of the jump. As a general rule of thumb going from an "open" to a "compressed" canter, the most open canter is needed for the open water, less for a triple bar, even less for an oxer, and the most compressed canter for a vertical. Terrain also impacts your pace: Downhill landings or landings in water require a more compressed canter than an uphill jump or one on consistent ground.

• *Direction:* Direction is possibly the most important component here. Without it, you're not going to jump the fence. Regardless of width and poll, you must be able to place your horse exactly where you'd like. Accuracy is paramount.

• *Balance:* Balance is last but not least important. Regardless of energy or pace your horse must be well balanced. The most common flaw occurs when the rider sends her horse more forward on a longer stride. You must keep in mind that you should maintain the horse's balance in this process. Most people resort to throwing the reins at their horse to allow him to move more forward. However, while you do lengthen his stride, his balance also suffers. Picture this as a constant state of falling forward, rather than striding out and in balance. You don't want to have the horse transfer some weight to his front end: All of the horse's power comes from what's behind the rider, and it is what propels him. Pulling you along with his front end will never produce a good jump, nor will it allow for much adjustment.

tip *Remember, less is more. A common affliction with riders is they'd like to control every step. Allow your horse the freedom to make mistakes and learn. From this you will form a team, both looking for a great jump.*

Running Out

What Happens

Rather than spending the energy to jump the fence, the horse finds a way to pop a shoulder and drift enough to go around it. Ultimately, unless you become more particular about his straightness, he will not form the habit of jumping, regardless of your approach.

Running out is the worst habit you come across when jumping. It can be very difficult to overcome. However, with a few quick tips you should be able to get your horse straightened out quickly. You need to understand that when he runs out he is ignoring your *turning* or *guiding* aids.

Especially important for event horses, riding a straight line has become the most important skill when on cross-country in recent years. Due to ever-improving riding and better horses, course designers are including more and more narrow fences and angles to separate the good from the best. This evolution does have its advantages: The complexes might be becoming more technically demanding but they are safer. Often the "skinny" fence or corner jump will be set on a slightly long distance, requiring a forward ride, which requires you to be able to gallop to it with confidence that your horse will not waver. Riding "backward" or "picking down" to the fence will assure you of a run out due to the striding between the two elements.

Why is running out so bad? When a horse has the propensity to run out, you have two main problems as you approach a scary or technical fence. First, will he stop? Second, will he run out? Even worse, he begins to run out, and due to his speed does not have time to get completely around the fence. Out of desperation, he then jumps. This will put you in the worst of all situations. As this happens he is much more likely to "hang a leg" meaning the inside front leg doesn't

Jumping a Single, Upright Barrel

Just as a point of reference, our event horses at Intermediate Level and above frequently jump a single barrel standing on end (figs. III.1 A–H).

How is this taught? Well it's not magic. You have to be precise with the jumps you jump. When your horse drifts, correct it! Starting with a normal-width fence—ours are 10 to 12 feet in width—jump it straight on, that is completely straight—90 degrees from the rail. As he gains confidence and consistency, start to introduce a small angle on the takeoff and landing. This angle should progress to the point where you are jumping at a 45-degree angle to the rail. Assuming this goes well, you can now introduce "skinny" rails (anything 6 feet or less in width). Again, from this point, continue down to skinnier and skinnier fences. Start with two barrels standing on end and finally down to one with a skinny pole on top, and then just the barrel standing alone.

III.1 A–H When jumping an upright barrel, you begin the process with a narrow rail on top. This can be made easier by adding a second barrel for solid width; a longer rail for more jumpable space; and a ground rail to help your horse read the fence better. Regardless of how wide, you must be completely accurate with your approach and landing. Any deviation must be fixed upon landing.

This first sequence shows Running Order jumping the barrel with a four-foot skinny rail placed on top (A–C). The following shows the final product, an arrow-straight approach and jump over a single standing barrel (D–G). Make sure to pat your horse after a good effort (H).

get picked up as quickly as the outside, hitting the rail and potentially flipping your horse in the process.

▶ Cause One

On your approach to a jump, your horse ducks out of the jump just before taking off. This is a clear example of his straightness not being maintained and the horse using his "crookedness" to evade the jump. You must be creative in your approach to solving this problem and find a way to control his body without restricting his forward motion.

Solution A

The root of all straightness problems lies in your horse's flatwork. Really, jumping should just be considered flatwork where a jump happens to get in the way. I've covered similar problems earlier in the text. Figure out which direction he likes to drift most often and work on suppling exercises that will increase his sensitivity to the aids so you can counteracting this habit of running out (see my recommendations for leg-yielding, p. 76).

III.2 A–C Drifting: In this sequence, Running Order clearly begins to pop his shoulder and drift to my left. Starting in photo C, notice my opening right rein, which I continue until the "popped" shoulder is back under control in F. Aside from the opening rein, I am also using a significant amount of left leg to help push his withers to the right. Ideally I'd like to have his poll, withers, and hips in a nearly straight line.

Solution B

So let's get this problem straightened out—literally. I've already said that when you present your horse to a jump, he must go...or else! Now, you have to become more specific. It's not good enough just to get to the other side, you must be accurate. If you were to place a coin on the top rail of a fence you should be able to jump centered exactly over it. This attention to detail must be maintained even when you are jumping a 12- or 16-foot-wide fence. Pick a specific point on the jump and jump it. Period.

Solution C

You need to have a straight approach and straight departure from each fence. This is especially important with a green horse that is learning to jump. The moment you allow him to waver before—or after—the jump, he will learn to drift at the moment of takeoff, which pushes him to the right or left in the air. This drift will tend to produce a horse that twists in the air and one that subsequently does not jump as clean or powerful as he could.

This is not to say that you can never jump a fence on an angle, but when doing so, your horse must remain straight between your leg and hand. You are looking to have your horse's hips completely square to the line over the jump. Any crookedness will produce a subpar effort.

Drifting

What Happens

Drifting happens just as your horse takes off. He pushes off harder with one hind leg than the other, thrusting his body to the right or left in the air.

Straightness is one of the key components of good jumping. When your horse approaches the fence crookedly or he drifts, a portion of his energy that could be used to elevate him well above the fence is instead devoted to pushing his body sideways (figs. III.2 A–G and III.3 A–C). In addition, not being straight makes it impossible for him to get the full advantage and use of his head and neck, as well as jump with a free hind end. Many horses will end up tucking their hind end rather than unhinging their pelvis over the fence for fear of hitting the rail.

III.3 A–C Corrected drift: In this attempt you can see how much straighter Running Order is through his body. I am still riding on a curved path, with a slight opening rein to help initiate the right turn upon landing. Also, note the exaggerated aid for the right lead upon landing. I am stepping into my left stirrup (C) with my upper body centered, allowing the most amount of freedom possible for his inside hind to step forward, thus ensuring the right lead. Remember the hind end is the key to your success.

▶ **Cause One**

Your horse does not stay straight as he jumps each jump. This can have its roots in a training or physical issue. First rule out the physical issues, and then address the training at hand.

Solution A

If you have a horse that is getting a bit older and has begun to drift more now than in years past, it's probably worth having your vet take a look at him. It is very possible that he has some joint pain that could be successfully managed thus enabling you to have a happy horse for years to come. Catching this sort of thing early is key to a horse's longevity.

Solution B

Solutions to most jumping problems begin with flatwork. Before I jump a horse, I devote a considerable amount of time making sure that my horse is forward in front of my leg, straight in his body, and stretching over his topline. When I do start jumping, all of this training must remain over fences.

When you start to transition to jumping, introduce cavalletti in your flatwork, which are nothing more than raised ground poles that you can progressively make bigger until your horse is actually jumping them. These can be randomly jumped during your flatwork in your dressage saddle. They are not big enough to worry about your horse's long-term soundness due to pounding. I jump them on a daily basis until they are no issue in the least.

▶ **Cause Two**

Many riders do not realize how inaccurate they are in their approach to a fence.

Solution A

Start off jumping a simple vertical with a long approach (at least six perfectly straight strides before the fence) and adequate room for a straight getaway on landing. It's vitally important to make sure that your horse is always straight on takeoff, in the air and on landing. *Do not* turn in the air. This is especially important with a younger horse whose jumping style is not yet confirmed.

Solution B

First start in sitting trot on a long approach—at least 15 to 20 meters before the jump. Find a ground person who can stand behind the fence to point out when you deviate from your planned line. You'll be very surprised how difficult it is to remain perfectly straight. Once this is accomplished, move on to the canter.

At the canter, things happen more quickly and corrections have to be implemented earlier to just keep yourself on your line! Your goal here is to be able to canter to the fence, keeping your body well centered, and be able to land on whichever lead you'd like, and halt in a straight line. Again, you'll be surprised how difficult this can be.

Solution C

Once you've got your single jump ironed out, move on to a hunter-type jumping course (that is, one with wide turns and straight approaches of six strides or more). Plan some long approaches (six or more strides) to a single or related line of four to six strides. Much like the single jump, you're looking to jump each fence as straight as possible. Progress to bending lines and tighter combinations—one to three strides.

During these exercises your horse will inevitably drift. When this occurs, correct by riding him forward and straight rather than steering him out of it with your hands. Steer with your legs. You don't want him to look like a drunken sailor!

▶ Cause Three

In this example, I'm going to deal with a horse that drifts to the *left* over a fence. A lot of riders react to this drift by pulling on the *right* rein. Very quickly they find themselves with a *right* drift requiring the *left* rein to correct it! This vicious cycle continues and will get worse the longer they attempt to remain on the straight line. It's very much how a rollover car accident happens. Overcorrecting can be fatal.

Solution

Rather than pulling the right rein to turn right, open it and at the same time, apply both legs with a 70/30 split: This means, of the hypothetical 100 pounds your legs can exert on your horse, use 70 pounds of it on your left side and 30 pounds on the right. Imagine you are trying to push the horse's left shoulder toward his right ear.

When the steering comes from your legs, you will notice the fix will be quicker, longer-lasting and you'll avoid an over-correction. The beauty of using your legs will also be that by the time you get to the jump you'll have plenty of energy, and your horse will jump out of his skin! Because he's straight, he will be able to fully utilize all of the energy available to him.

Course Strategy

For the best odds of jumping well in competition, follow these few pieces of advice.

• *Walk and study the course.* You should know every minute detail and nuance. The course designer is asking a series of questions, so make sure you have them answered *before* entering the ring.

• *Watch!* Study the course being ridden by as many people as possible. You will get the most benefit if you can find horses that have similar strides and tendencies to your own. Some lines can ride shorter or longer than you expect. Don't be caught by surprise.

• *Debrief yourself.* Following your round, analyze what went well and what could be improved. If possible, I will often go back and walk distances that didn't ride as expected to effectively calibrate myself with my horse.

• *Use video!* This is the most valuable tool at your disposal. There is nothing like watching your performance. Unlike a trainer or friend telling you what happened, you believe what you see. You can analyze a video to death and your bad habits will be gone before you know it! In show jumping, even when trying to ride fast in a jump off, remember to land straight. Turning in the air may help you a great deal for the technical aspects seen in cross-country, but it will tend to cost you a rail in the show ring: The moment you attempt to turn, your horse will begin to drop his hind end in anticipation.

▶ Cause Four

When the horse is drifting to the left, the other typical response by a rider is to use a pulley rein on the right because the horse doesn't seem to be responding. The downfall here is that the horse, all of the sudden, has a "rubber neck"; he bends his head right and pops his shoulder left, making the problem worse.

Solution

The fix is the same as mentioned in Cause Three (p. 142). Your legs, along with an opening rein, will give you a lasting fix.

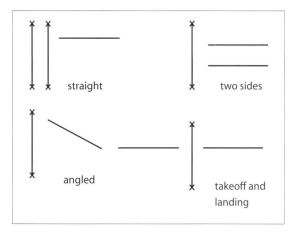

Diagram 4

Places to set poles on the ground, before and after the jump, for the horse that drifts to the left.

▶ Cause Five

Your horse can have a natural tendency to drift over the fence, one that is *not* caused by the rider, but instead might be the result of a physical weakness or soreness.

Solution A

I often place rails to better explain to the horse what's expected (Diagram 4). In the case of the drifting horse, set a rail on the landing side of the fence parallel to the direction you're jumping the fence (figs. III.4 A–C). I start with the rail near the standard, and move it inward proportionally to the degree of drifting.

With a greener or careful horse I start wider and work it in. If you start with the pole too far in toward the middle of the jump, you risk landing on the rail and dealing a blow to your horse's confidence.

Solution B

Aside from a landing pole on one side (the side the horse is trying to drift toward), you can also use two poles from the ground to the highest jump rail that come to a point at the center of the jump (figs. III.5 A–C). This will act to funnel your horse in the middle, and make him less dependent on you to guide him perfectly straight. This exercise is also good for horses that are slower with

III.4 A–C This is the most common configuration that I use (A). This particular setup is for a horse that drifts to the left. I've provided a front view of what you, the rider, would see on approach to this configuration (B). I also use the "two-sides" setup on occasion because it forces the horse to land in a straight line. It's often useful with horses that twist over the jump (C).

III.5 A–C In A and B you see the standard configuration for V poles, front and side views. Photo C is a lesser used configuration. It tends to create a rounder bascule over a fence. It's especially useful for a horse that is not as flexible in his hips on the downside of the jump.

III.6 A–E Tie a knot in the reins by placing both reins together, and while holding the loop in your left hand, insert the buckle through with your right (A). To tighten, pull with your right hand, bracing the knot with your left (B). The knot should be short enough to allow you to drop the reins without a significant slack in them (C–E).

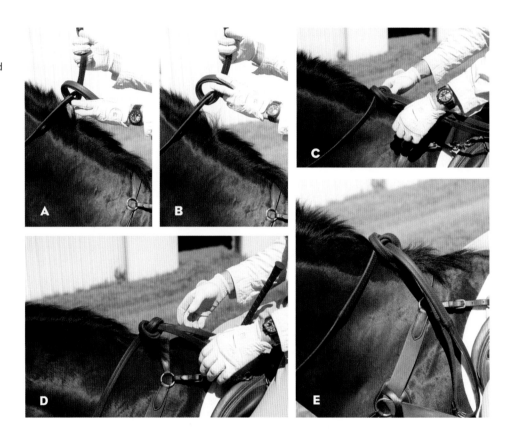

their front end or are not tight with their knees. The same rule of thumb should be applied, start wide and work more narrow. Just make sure that the ground end of the poles stays roughly the width of the standards. If the funnel gets too narrow, you significantly increase your chance of an accident.

▶ **Cause Six**

The rider does not have the ability to steer the horse with her legs. (The most common cause of a horse's problems is the rider!)

Solution A

The best tool I've found to force a rider to steer with her legs is a simple knot in the reins (figs. III.6 A–E). Take the slack end of your reins and tie them in a knot—quite short. Start your single jump with a long approach and you'll probably find that your horse doesn't drift nearly as much as he did just a minute earlier. Now you are steering with your legs!

III.7 A–H This photo sequence demonstrates how a raked approach is created. I start by raking the footing on the approach side of the jump (A & B).

Now riding it, I'm turning into the approach and being very careful to primarily use my outside aids to prevent Running Order from popping his shoulder left, or conversely, swinging his haunches out (C).

I'm nearly straight, still concentrating on channeling him forward toward the jump into a forgiving hand (D).

During this straight portion, I'm looking to maintain the straightness I was able to establish earlier, as well as keep his rhythm and balance the same (E & F).

Just on takeoff, I begin to ask for the left lead so that he has ample time to jump through with his left hind and land in a good balance. If I were to pull on the left rein for the lead, it would tend to produce a twist or drift in his bascule (G).

This is the final result so you can go back and check your approach. When the ground is first raked, it's very clear if you've succeeded or failed. The same holds true for after the fence, as well (H).

Solution B

I've always found a visual very helpful for learning. Start with a freshly dragged arena. Find a rake to drag a line in the footing directly to the center of the jump and beyond. Your goal is to canter down this line, jump your jump and continue in the rake's path (figs. III.7 A–H).

Stopping/Refusing

What Happens

Stopping might be the second on the list of worst jumping habits. You find yourself on a good approach to a fence, but at the last moment, your horse locks the brakes up and doesn't jump the fence.

Whether it's from the horse's lack of confidence or the rider's ability to "explain the question," your horse will stop when he feels it's not safe to jump the jump (fig. III.8). Rarely do you find a purely malicious horse that stops out of spite. Most stop as a result of frequent bad experiences when jumping.

III.8 Following our approach, PJ takes exception to the Liverpool and refuses to jump.

▶ Cause One

A horse stops for many reasons, but in most cases the root cause lies in the fact that your horse is not sufficiently in *front of your leg*. Despite a lot of effort on your part, this lack of responsiveness gives you little in results. In an ideal world, you should be approaching a fence with your horse gently drawing you to it; by no means do you want him dragging you to the fence, but it certainly should feel as if it's his idea (figs. III.9 A & B)

Solution A

How is this accomplished? Through tuning! Before you even start to think of jumping, make sure your horse is in front of your leg. To repeat, rehashing the building blocks of riding, use light leg to ask your horse to move forward. If you don't get an instant response, ask again using the same light pressure, but this time with the help of your whip. It is absolutely critical that you don't use all the leg pressure you can exert just to get your horse to walk, trot or canter.

Timing should not be overlooked. On approach your horse will have a moment when he begins to suck back or drop behind your leg—usually three to five strides from the jump. You have to be lightning quick to respond; a stride after he begins to suck back, he will also begin to lose straightness. If you use your leg or crop at the very first moment, your horse will still be straight and your encouragement more effective. A moment late, you'll end up driving him forward on a line that's not square to the jump, thereby making the effort even more difficult!

III.9 A & B These photos show the approach to a fence from just about two strides away. Notice I am in a neutral balance with a soft contact. I'm allowing Running Order to gently take the rein with his nose out slightly so he can evaluate the fence. Don't confuse the nose being out with him being strung out. Look at his hind end: He is clearly well engaged and in an appropriate balance to jump the fence.

III.10 A–F Far from the fence, I am looking to place PJ in an appropriate balance, pace, and direction for the jump ahead (A).

As he begins to look, it feels as if he is sucking back or falling behind my leg (B).

I move into a more defensive position, with my weight shifted toward the rear in an attempt to drive him forward (C).

At this point I'm in trouble. He has been able to pop his left shoulder, pitching him on the forehand and allowing him to dig in and begin to stop (D).

We're nearly stopped at this point; notice my position: lower leg forward and shoulders tall (E). This allows all of my weight to fall into my heel preventing me from going over his ears!

Now that he is stopped, I'm doing my best to keep him straight. Even in the moment he stopped, he wanted to run to the left of the fence. I made sure we stopped in front and I turned him to the right. Always choose the opposite direction of where your horse wanted to go (F).

Solution B

Aside from your leg you have another natural aid that is often underutilized. When jumping I like to use a light two-point seat as the *neutral* state of riding. But if you want to drive your horse forward, simply shift your weight back. This can be something as simple as a very slight weight shift while remaining in the two-point. Or, taking it to the other extreme, you sit down and drive your horse forward.

When I'm riding a horse that is "chicken" or green, I will tune him into my weight as much as my leg. Simply, pick up a canter around the perimeter of the ring in your neutral two-point position. Make a distinct shift in your balance backward to drive your horse forward. It's likely that nothing will happen the first time,

so at this point, you have to teach him this weight shift is an aid just like your leg, and an aid that warrants a response (figs. III.10 A–F). Again, go back to the neutral position, shift your weight back and give him a tap with your crop. If this isn't sufficient, move on to a swift hit (see sidebar, p. 152).

The same procedure should be taught to your horse when you assume the driving-seat position. The end goal is to have another aid that you can use in a pinch to get your horse to the other side of the fence. The second benefit here is that you can use a lesser weight shift to make small adjustments where adding your leg might be too much of a disturbance.

The place where this can come in handy is when show jumping. If your horse begins to spook off a jump during the approach, you can shift your weight slightly back. This will send your horse forward, but in a moderate way—enough to overcome his fear but not enough to send him careening into the jump.

Stop by your local lower-level event or horse show and watch the introductory levels. I can assure you, you'll see more examples than we'd like to admit where a horse begins to spook and the rider goes overboard with leg aids and drives him right into the fence. The horse does not stop, so I guess that's the upside, but he also manages to dislodge every rail in the process.

Remember, for your horse to jump well he must be as relaxed as possible, and he must have time to process what the jump is asking him to do with his body—that is, enough time to not only recognize what is being asked, but also to adjust his body accordingly to allow him to jump clean. Most horses want to jump well, you just have to get them to the jump in a relaxed, straight and energetic fashion.

A Successful Jump Following a Refusal

Before even approaching the fence I tune PJ up to my leg. With light pressure, he should jump forward.

When he doesn't, my leg is applied a second time along with a sharp hit from the crop (figs. III.11 A–F).

Notice the defensive position with my legs solidly on two strides prior to the jump in A. I'm much more aggressive this time, certain he's going to try to stop.

In B, my lower leg-position is still in a secure location, so if he were to stop, I'd still be in the tack. Take note of the soft contact: I'm not restricting his head and neck. Seeing that he responded well to my leg in the previous frame, I did not need to use my crop for additional support. Had he been less responsive, I would have, without a doubt!

Again, I'm taking great care not to allow my upper body to get ahead of the motion, and stay well-balanced, with a soft, following hand in C and D.

I am still slightly behind the motion in E, but again making sure not to catch him in the mouth midflight. My goal is not to give him any reason to make jumping an unpleasant experience.

Due to the strong ride approaching the jump, PJ has over-compensated by jumping slightly flat in F. This has sent him farther than normal on the back side. If this had been a combination, I would have had to make sure to steady him seeing that the distance gets tight quickly. I'm making all efforts to continue allowing him to use his head and neck by maintaining a straight-line elbow to bit, with a soft hand.

▶ **Cause Two**

A lot of horses stop at one particular type of fence rather than all fences. Prime examples are a Liverpool in show jumping (fig. III.12) and a ditch in eventing (see figs. III.14 A–F, p. 156). The horse often refuses out of fear—called "fear-stopping."

Solution A

Horses remember a bad experience and forever associate it with the type of jump where it occurred. So it's very important to introduce scary-type fences early in their training—on a small scale. I have horses jumping a Liverpool within the first week or two of learning to jump. It may be only one foot wide, but it's there. The same is true for ditches, banks and water.

When teaching a horse for the first time and you are not sure of him, override the fence. Your job is to get him to the other side at all costs, even if he jumps it like a water buffalo or as if his tail is on fire. Be ready with your crop, and even if he slightly hesitates, react! Remember, you have no limit on the number of times you can jump the fence other than daylight. If he scoots over it, or even

III.12 A Liverpool in show-jumping competition.

III.13 A side view of the setup that allows you to longe the horse over a jump without snagging the line on the jump standard.

bolts, calmly circle around for another attempt. For each of the next few approaches, look to use fewer driving aids so that he just takes you to the fence—without issue—on a light contact and very little leg.

Solution B

If you don't feel confident or have not had much success in the saddle, you always have the option of longeing your horse over the fence.

Exercise

1 Find some jump standards that are short enough not to catch the longe line. I also place a pole with one end on the ground and the other end on the top of both the standards so that the longe line will be able to slide up the poles and end up on the landing side of the jump (III.13). The last thing you need is a jump standard tangled in the longe line and being dragged by your bolting horse.

2 You should prepare him just as if you were riding. Tune him into your clucking sound by reinforcing with the whip. This will come in handy when you need to add that last bit of encouragement before he jumps. Once he's longeing well, add the jump itself.

▶ **Cause Three**

Continuing on with the Liverpool example, let's say your horse has come to you with a fear of jumping this type of fence. I've got good news and bad news for you. The situation can be improved and your horse will learn to jump it, but the fear is never going to completely disappear. Anyone telling you otherwise is just out for your money! This horse is always going to have an eye out for this "deadly" vinyl trap.

Solution A

So first make sure this horse is responsive enough to your leg. Start off just cantering around the ring, asking him to move on with a light leg. You need him to shoot out in front of you with your lightest leg aid. Try visualization: While riding without a girth or breastplate, imagine putting your leg on and your horse scooting out from under you, with you landing on your butt on the ground as your horse gallops away! This is what you should expect to feel when he is very responsive. Your goal is to know what you need to do to make him this sensitive.

Solution B

With that in mind, the next step is to create the same sensation while jumping. Most likely you won't have problems with a "normal" sort of fence. Warm him up over ordinary jumps to make sure that he's jumping well, then tune him up to your leg and seat while jumping. In this example, let's say that though the horse is normally jumping 3 foot 3 inches, he wants no part of any Liverpool. A typical sliding stop is what you get when you attempt this jump.

Exercise

1 Your plan is as follows. Set up your Liverpool's height to 2 feet 6 inches, with a ground pole in front and behind the tarp to create a concrete boundary. Place another jump somewhere else in the arena that will allow you a flowing jumping sequence before the Liverpool. This jump should be an ascending oxer, roughly 3 feet tall with the front rail a few holes lower than the back rail.

tip *Keep in mind that although a sliding stop into the jump is bad, even worse would be a half attempt at jumping where he begins to take off, gets his front legs over the top rail and decides jumping isn't all it's cracked up to be. You are soon flying backward, with rails and legs tangled together, dirt flying into the vinyl (the ground covering that simulates water) scaring your horse to death. You may have thought you had a big problem on your hands before, but you're in for a real "treat" now! Stay committed even if you feel your horse starting to suck back. Don't give up halfway, because you could very well make the problem worse.*

2 Canter to the oxer at an appropriate pace. Roughly two strides away from the jump, shift your weight back into more of a driving position, and add a light leg aid at the same time as you sternly use your whip. Your horse should bolt forward. Bear in mind that if he is hypersensitive, he may jump flat causing a rail to come down. When he comes around one more time to repeat the process, do it this time without the use of the whip. Your goal here is to give him an "over-confident" feeling over the jump.

3 The next time around, shift your weight back and add your leg. If he jumps forward don't reinforce with your stick, but anything less from him than a response that gives you whiplash should be countered with your stick. Even though this jump is not the problem, you need to lay the groundwork to tune him so finely into your aids that they overpower any desire he has to do a reining-style sliding stop into the Liverpool.

4 So you're all set: Your horse is bounding forward just from your "thought" of sending him forward. You're all ready to give it a go! Just after jumping the oxer continue cantering around the ring for a long straight approach to the Liverpool. Six strides from the jump, sit back with your weight all anchored in your lower legs: your heels, down and forward with your leg on, and your whip at the ready position.

The Second Time Can Be Worse Than the First

One quick note to remember, especially with spooky horses, is that the second time over the same jump can be worse than the first. You most often see this with ditches, where the horse does not realize there is a ditch until he is on top of it the first time around (figs. III.14 A–F). The second time you approach the same ditch, don't be caught off guard. Your horse is well aware of what's coming this time, so I strongly recommend riding harder. Just like jumps in the ring, circle around and head to the ditch again. The key to your horse learning and retaining the information is to allow him time to process what is being asked. When in doubt, do it again. You can never expose your horse to too much.

5 I also assume a half-bridge rein position (p. 104) so that you can take your hand off the rein should you need to reinforce your leg and seat aids. The closer you get to the Liverpool, the stronger your legs become. All happens quickly, but if you even sense a slight reservation or sucking back from the horse, get your whip out and use it! Remember, in this scenario you're not going to get in trouble for over-riding. Plan to give him a smack on takeoff regardless. If you get over on this attempt, then great! Come back around and progressively come with lighter and lighter driving aids until you can just "point and shoot"!

6 If that didn't work, go back to the oxer and repeat the set-up process. At the same time, ask a person on the ground to drop the Liverpool's height to a cross rail or one-foot vertical, roll the Liverpool vinyl so it is narrower, and try the whole process again. If this doesn't work (which, without a doubt, it should!) then drop

III.14 A–F This is Darby's first attempt at jumping a ditch. I am trying my best to approach on a straight line with plenty of energy and a slightly defensive body position (A).

As she begins to spook I am well back with my upper body and I'm able to still drive her forward and try to get her back going straight as a result (B).

With my right leg on, she hops over the ditch (C).

Obviously, I'm still well behind her, but I'm doing my best to regain balance without the use of the reins to support my weight. I find this especially difficult seeing that she is all of 15 hands and I'm 6 foot 3 (D)!

Our second attempt goes much more smoothly, but note that I have the reins in a half-bridge in my left hand and my crop at the ready in my right; if she had "looked" I could have quickly acted (E & F).

the rail so it's just lying on the ground. If you have no luck with this then you're going to have to seek the advice of a professional trainer who you hope will be able to hop on and get the dirty work done for you. Not jumping the Liverpool is *not* an acceptable result!

7 Assuming that now your horse is jumping the Liverpool, progressively increase its difficulty. The trick with training horses is to know when, and how much, to push the envelope. You're guaranteed not to progress when you don't push your comfort level, but "blowing it out of the water" is only going to force you to take a few steps back. Horses will find a way to progress at their own speed, whether you want them to or not.

▶ **Cause Four**

Now that you have fear-stopping under control, what other factors contribute to horses stopping? Often when teaching clinics, I hear, "Well he's usually very good, but every once in a while he decides he doesn't like a particular jump," or "Every once in a while he stops, but I circle around and he goes the second time. So it's really not that big of a deal." It *is* a big deal—it's a deal breaker!

Solution

A horse is a creature of habit; he doesn't wake up on the wrong side of the bed one day and decide he doesn't like blue paint. Riders who make these sort of remarks generally don't realize that their horse is behind their leg and under-powered. It's very important to have an educated eye on the ground to identify whether your horse is energetic enough, or not.

When jumping, your horse should also be *drawing* you slightly forward, and on the lightest leg aid, go more forward with conviction. It's very important not to ride with a looped rein, or inconsistent contact. The moment the rein loops you have no means of communication and you'll receive no advanced warning that your horse is sucking back and about to stop.

I like to think that when approaching a jump he should be actively looking to jump it and drawing you to it. Hypothetically, let's say you are riding with a contact weighing 3 pounds, but the moment that force goes down to 2½ pounds,

III.15 A–E In the first photos, Conor is pulling me forward because I'm pinching with my knees, which are acting as a pivot point. I'm quickly being pulled out of position and relying on Running Order's neck for support (A–D). In the last photo, Conor is pulling again, but this time my knee is slightly open allowing the force to fall into my heel and my upper body to remain in place. To prepare as the rein's pulling force begins to escalate, I'm tightening my core, staying tall, and allowing my heels to sink (E).

you need to get your foot on the gas pedal! When you can keep that constant 3 pounds of contact weight, you'll never have a problem.

▶ **Cause Five**

What other contributing factor can increase the chance your horse will stop? Let's focus on your position. Your lower leg is your foundation and it can have a dramatic effect on your horse, not only when inadvertently using your heel or spur, but also how it influences your upper body. A weak lower leg is unacceptable when jumping; much attention and effort must be made to improve it (figs. III.15 A–E).

Solution

The solution lies in improving your jumping position. See the photo series on p. 161 (figs. III.16 A & B) and look at the upcoming position photos in this chapter.

▶ **Cause Six**

Some horses have been rushed or overfaced. In these cases, a horse is being asked to jump larger or more intimidating fences than he feels comfortable doing. He will often exhibit nervousness and apprehension as well as abnormal sweating, and when he does stop at a fence, he can demonstrate panic-type behavior, for example, running backward or making other unpredictable movements.

Solution

It's very important to take a number of training steps back. Lower your expectations and the height of the fences to a point where the horse is able to jump without issues. When you can determine this level of competence, slowly begin

A Learning Experience

I was called by "Leo's" owner, Jen Dermody, one summer day. She had a talented jumper that had tossed her a few times and was obviously not confident in his ability and quite spooky. I assured her that I was certain we could figure something out to help. She brought him over, and after warming up, I cantered toward a one-foot-high gate fence. I was about a stride out from the fence when, before I could blink, I was flossing my teeth in his mane!

Jen had warned me, but I never thought he'd be as quick as this. The fix took a few months, but I basically started small and rode aggressively. Soon we were able to jump around a small course without much of an issue. I always kept in mind how quick he could be, so on the approach to each jump, I kept my shoulders back and prepared to use my whip when needed. The next step was not to raise the fences but to make them as "scary" as

possible. This is where we had to be creative. Anything and everything was dragged out of the barn to jump: muck tubs, sheets, coolers, flowers, fake rocks, jackets, the list was endless.

Of course, with each new addition, Leo questioned whether this was really a good idea. I assured him it was, and soon enough, we were again jumping around well. Just before raising the fences, I also introduced jumping at angles and very tight rollback turns. This made it more difficult for Leo, seeing that he had less time to see the jump, which increased its shock factor. He handled things well and the jumps' height increased—as did his placings. That summer he was winning classes containing 80 or more entries at HITS Saugerties. What initially deterred him—his spookiness—ended up being his best virtue. He was incredibly careful and could jump just about anything—from anywhere and at any angle.

to increase the jumps' complexity and height. Continue on for as long as the nervous behavior is not present.

Rider Ineffectiveness While Jumping

What Happens

Many jumping problems stem from flaws in the rider's equitation. Without a solid base of support and a balanced position, the rider can end up negatively influencing the horse.

▶ **Cause One:** *The Lower Leg*

The most common flaw seen in a rider's lower leg results in a position known as the "chair seat." This occurs when the lower leg is placed well in front of the body (figs. III.16 A). Remember, ideally, a straight line should be able to be drawn from your shoulder to your hip to your heel. The chair seat tends to put people behind the motion over a jump. When this happens, the rider often will end up using her reins for balance. The horse soon is hesitant to jump, knowing that the moment he takes off, he's going to get popped in the mouth.

Solution

One very easy self-test can be performed at the trot. When posting, simply change your diagonal by standing for two beats rather than sitting. If your lower

III.16 A & B In A, my lower legs are too far forward, placing me in the "chair-seat." Notice the extended lower leg and weight distribution to the rear. This position will leave me left "behind" when my horse jumps, as well as hollow his back and cause me to pull on his mouth. In B I'm demonstrating the correct lower-leg jumping position, which allows neutral balance.

III.17 A–E Earlier, I discussed "pinching" at the knee while standing; now I'm demonstrating pinched knees while jumping (A). My pinched knees have eliminated any base of support. In turn, my upper body has become ahead of the motion (B). Farther into the horse's bascule, notice an even greater loss of balance (C). Upon landing things have not improved; I will not be able to influence my horse for a few strides due to my lack of balance (D).

tip *Where might the chair-seat position actually be advantageous? It can come in handy for short periods of time either with a "dirty" stopper, or over a massive drop fence. In both cases, you have a rapidly decelerating horse beneath you, so this seat can increase your odds of staying on top, when all is said and done. You must remember when you're left behind at a jump, to allow the reins to slip through your fingers (fig. III.11D, p. 152). This gives the horse full freedom to use his head and neck. He will jump better for it.*

leg is too far forward you will fall backward out of control. You should be able to change your diagonal "up" and remain light in the seat (fig. III.16 B)

The same principle can be tested at the canter: To the canter's beat, alternatively stand and sit without using any reins for balance.

▶ **Cause Two:** *Pinching with the Knees*

The second most commonly seen jumping flaw occurs when a rider pinches with the knees over the fence (figs. III.17 A–D). This has the opposite effect on the rider's body, throwing the lower leg back and the upper body forward onto the horse's neck, causing the rider to be ahead of the motion. In addition to overweighting your horse's forehand making jumping more difficult, getting ahead like this will also limit your ability to influence the horse on the other side of the fence.

Solution A

When approaching a fence try to imagine keeping a space between your knee and the saddle. By turning your knee out, your weight should drop into your heel and significantly strengthen your base of support.

III.17 E I'm demonstrating the proper "driving" grip.

Lower Leg Struggles

I am tall, 6 feet 3 inches, with a long leg. This, of course, can be a tremendous asset to a rider, but for about a year-and-a-half, it was my downfall. I went through a period of falling off: I hit the dirt several times in competition in a year (not to mention all the falls on other occasions).

Thankfully, for many of these falls I was fortunate to have a video. The first few I wrote off as freak incidents, but as they continued, as stubborn as I was at the time, I could no longer ignore the facts. I sat down and watched fall after fall in slow motion. I also clicked over to YouTube to find videos of Andrew Nicholson and William Fox-Pitt, both extremely talented riders and both quite tall who had to deal with the same issues as me.

There was a clear difference: If the horse's bascule starts at 3 o'clock and finishes at 9

o'clock, at the 2 o'clock position I would begin to pinch with my knees and commit my upper body prematurely. Because of this, a stop or a disturbance caused by the horse hitting the jump sent my lower legs even farther back and, in turn, my upper body over the front, which caused me to fall.

When watching the videos of the others, I could see that, if anything, their lower legs or heels moved farther forward toward the jump at the beginning of takeoff. Their upper body remained still and it allowed the horse to "jump up" to them. This way, even in a precarious situation, these riders remain solidly on top.

I worked very hard over the subsequent months, and still do today, to perfect my leg position. I am always trying to maximize the benefits my tall height offers without falling into its weaknesses!

Solution B

Your lower leg can be improved through a few, very simple jumping exercises. The best I've found is to change your grip on the reins over to a "driving" configuration (fig. III.17 E.) When your horse takes off, spread your hands wide so that you are not able to use the neck for balance. The driving grip will feel strange initially, but you'll be shocked how much softer your hand will be—and your leg more secure—as a result.

For the novice rider, this exercise should be introduced in a gymnastic line in order to limit the variables. Later, the rein position can be implemented in an entire sequence of jumps. You'll soon find that it's impossible to have any movement in your lower leg while remaining balanced midflight or upon landing.

▶ Cause Three: *Upper-Body Position*

Now that the rider has a solid base of support, she often will allow her upper body to overcompensate for the size of the jump in one of two ways: by overfolding or by standing straight up. These body positions tend to alter a horse's balance and reduce the rider's ability to influence him in a positive way, before and after the jump (figs. III.18 A–E).

Solution

Imagine that the height of your eyes does not change before, during, or after a jump. It's much like how a skier's legs absorb a mogul: the lower body collapses and comes closer to the skier's core. The same should be true for the rider. Let the jump come to you rather than you to the jump.

Continuing with this line of thought, your shoulders have a significant influence over your balance and your effect on your horse's jump. Focus your eyes on the top rail of the jump until it disappears between your horse's ears, at which point he moves either to the next jump or to a focal point in the distance. The last place you want to be looking when your horse is about to take off is the ground (figs. III.19 A–I). Guess what! You'll end up where you are looking, and the ground isn't all that comfortable when you hit it at speed.

▶ Cause Four: *Rider Can't "See" a Distance to a Fence*

Riders often approach a jump with no idea whether they will arrive at a long, short, or perfect takeoff distance. Regardless of skill level, all riders can benefit from further refinement of their "eye."

Solution A

You can increase your odds dramatically of a successful jump if you approach each jump with the appropriate direction or line, energy, balance, and pace (see p. 134). Assuming you can consistently accomplish this, the next step is to begin to accurately place your horse at the desired takeoff distance.

Solution B

There are 101 different exercises to improve your eye; however, you'll be relieved that in this book, I'll narrow these down to my "top two."

III.18 A–E Overfolding or ducking: My upper body is already in contact with my horse's neck, destabilizing both my and his balance (A & B). Here, my head is obviously on the right side of his neck. This skewed balance will make a clear jump even more difficult (C). At this point, I'm still ahead, and I would not be able to react quickly to an unpredictable situation (D & E).

III.19 A–I This series shows correct jumping upper-body position: Notice that in each photo frame, my head is roughly the same distance from the ground.

Exercise

The *first* exercise is jumping on a circle where the jump does not have to be big.

1 Start with one cavalletti on a 20-meter circle. As you canter around approaching the jump, begin counting down when you recognize where you are relative to the jump. Most people find their distance roughly two to four strides from the fence. Soon, you'll get more and more comfortable identifying this earlier and earlier seeing that it will be at the same point in the circle each time around. As soon as you're able to get the same number of strides three times in a row, proceed to the next step.

2 When you identify where you are relative to the fence, look away. I'll take four strides from the jump for example. Have a friend stand in the center of the circle. When you see you are four strides away from the jump, turn your head so you're looking directly at your friend; don't turn your head back until after you've jumped the jump. This is very difficult to do at first.

The great thing about this exercise is that you begin to realize you don't have to continue to look at a jump once you know where you are. Your body has the remarkable ability to identify what's happening under it. If your horse begins to speed up, you'll be able to slow him down, or if he drifts in or out, you can straighten him and send him forward, or you can hold him to compensate. This is a very valuable tool that will greatly improve your courses: They will be much smoother now that you can begin to prepare for the jump that comes *after* the one in front of you—*before* you've even jumped the one in front of you!

The *second* exercise has two parts.

1 The first part, which I still find most difficult, is a progressive counting-down exercise. All you need for it is one jump that you can approach from either direction. Jump the first time and count down from one stride out. The second time, approach the jump from the other direction and count down from *two* strides out. Continue this until you're counting down up to *eight* strides from the fence.

> **tip** *Keep in mind your goal is to get the correct number of strides, of equal length, without disruptions. The correct number is a result of a positive, balanced approach. All too often, counting strides leads to the rider pulling on the horse in front of the fence in an attempt to fit it in the expected number. Don't fall into that trap! Counting up, rather than down, often helps reduce this tendency.*

2 This exercise sounds easier to execute than it is in real life! But it will help you immensely. Head out onto a jumping course where you count *eight* strides out from every jump; and also count *every* stride in each combination.

Jumping Theory and Execution: Seeing a Distance

How does tuning your eye actually help your performance? Let's use an example of two verticals set 60 feet apart in a straight line (fig. III.20). At this distance, your horse should take four strides in between: 6 feet for landing, four 12-foot strides, and 6 feet for takeoff.

But, the horse and rider team that jumps both fences in four strides has not necessarily succeeded. To jump effectively, a horse has to arrive at the jump with energy and balance, and most importantly, the rider must not actively be pulling on the reins when the horse needs to leave the ground.

Imagine Rider One who jumps into the combination with too much pace on a longer stride than ideal: she lands and takes three 14 foot strides leaving only 6 feet to squeeze the last stride in before the horse must take off again. While she "technically" got the four strides, her horse had a less than stellar experience and is probably contemplating why he jumped the jump. Next time around it could very well be a different story.

III.20 Keep in mind when jumping, you should look at the top rail until it passes between your horse's ears. Once it gets to this point, move your eye to your next jump or focal point.

Rider Two also comes in on the 14 foot stride, realizes her error and is able to correct the problem before the second jump. Her stride lengths are as follows: 14, 12, 10, and 12 feet. While not an ideal situation, she still arrives with a much better result at the second jump. The rider should have recognized that she was on too long of a stride *before* jumping the first element of the line. Luckily, she had enough time to make the correction, and was not in the horse's way by the last stride before the second element.

Rushing the Fence

What Happens

On an approach to a jump, your horse quickly accelerates when he's just a few strides from the fence. He often lands and gallops away from the fence, and the rider feels as if she has 100 pounds in her hand, with no effect.

▶ Cause One

Most riders deal with it by increasing the severity of the bit they are using in an attempt to hold the horse from "racing." However, from the horse's point of view, the rider is restricting his ability to clear the jump. Consequently, the horse feels unsure whether or not he can jump the fence without hitting it with his hind end. As a result, he speeds up at the last moment to make sure he leaves himself enough room. The more the rider tries to slow him the more the horse rushes to compensate.

III.21 An approach in a balanced, relaxed canter.

Solution

I know that it is counterintuitive, but you must allow the horse to go to the fence at a slightly increased pace in order to make progress. Your job is to instill confidence that you will not restrict his ability to jump the fence well. Rather than just going for a stronger bit, you're going to slow your horse down by altering the jump and the line.

Exercise

1 The best exercise for a horse like this is to jump a simple vertical on a 20 meter circle (fig. III.21). The moment he rushes at the fence you begin to turn him, landing on the circle after the fence. Many riders trying this exercise aren't quite comfortable with such a short approach so they are soon riding an oval, not a circle. However, you must be very careful to keep your figure accurate because inaccuracies just exacerbate the problem: The circle allows you to keep a consistent bend and pace while jumping., but on an oval, your horse will land and immediately "pop" his shoulder.

2 Use an *opening inside rein* (fig. III.22) to invite the horse to turn and a *supportive inside leg* to promote the inside bend. The key here is to actually turn in the air. It won't take too many circles for the horse to realize that there is no advantage to going faster because it only makes life more difficult on the back side of the fence. You can also play with the height of the fence; the more careful horses slow down when presented with a larger effort—that is, within reason.

III.22 This is an appropriate opening rein to invite a slight flexion to the inside.

3 Once you're able to keep a steady pace around the circle, intentionally move onto an oval with a straight approach and exit from the jump. In time, you're looking to stretch the oval as long as his pace does not change. Soon enough you'll be riding with a direct relationship between your inside leg and outside rein as if on a circle, but you'll be on a straight line with your pace unchanging.

If your horse regresses and begins to rush again, back on the circle you go! It's also very helpful to have an educated person on the ground. Often, what feels fast to you is actually not, and your objective observer (a moderator of sorts) will make sure you are holding up your end of the deal (you are not beginning to fall into your old habits of pulling).

▶ **Cause Two**

Some horses also rush because they are inadvertently being told to by the rider. The problem is that the rider is unaware of it. This is often the case with nervous or anxious riders who get tighter with their legs or tense in their bodies the closer they get to the jump.

Solution

While not an option for all, it might be best to take a lesson on an experienced, very quiet horse. This will allow you to concentrate solely on *you* rather than worrying about your horse.

III.23 The knot should be tight enough to allow you to completely drop the reins without any slack in them. You always want to make sure there is no chance of a horse's front end getting caught up.

You're going to have to work very hard to try and relax. If your horse is quiet enough, jumping a grid comprising a number fences might come in handy.

Exercise

1 Jump through the grid a few times to make sure your horse is familiar with it. From there, tie a knot in your reins so that you're able to drop the reins entirely, extending your arms outward like "wings" as you go through the grid (fig. III.23).

2 You can also head through the grid without stirrups. When you can leave your horse to the jumping and just concentrate on your own balance, the payoff will be great!

BONUS SECTION

The Pace of the Canter: How to Jump Different Types of Fences

In an ideal world, you need to establish the canter you'd like to have when approaching the jump at the midpoint in the turn before (Diagram 5). There is a limited number of types of jumps that you'll encounter, therefore, a limited number of pace and balance combinations you'd like to be able to quickly establish. Practice these so that, without thinking, you'll

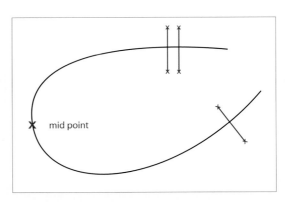

Diagram 5 Establish the correct canter midpoint in the turn before the jump.

III.24 A & B Verticals: Running Order jumping two different vertical fences in the show-jumping phase of the Rolex Kentucky CCI**** in 2012.

be able to quickly set yourself up for any type of jump. This is the key to jumping: With an appropriate approach, correct distances will just seem to appear. Nothing will be forced, and your horse will never jump better. Let's cover each type of fence.

III.25 A & B
Oxer: Wishfull-V at
the HITS Saugerties
in a 1.30 m class
in 2012 (A), and
Running Order at
the 2012 CCI**** in
Kentucky (B).

Show Jumps

• *Vertical* A vertical is about the most basic type of fence you'll find (figs. III.24 A & B). Horses should jump this out of a *medium* pace. The canter must be active, consistent and well balanced.

• *Oxer* An oxer can be *ascending* or *square,* which means, respectively, the front rail is either lower or at the same height as the back rail (figs. III.25 A & B). The width of an oxer can change dramatically. A taller, narrower oxer tests your horse's power; lower and wider ones encourage your horse to stretch over his topline, producing a rounder jump. An oxer should be jumped in a balance similar to the vertical jumps but on a slightly more open stride. It is much easier for your horse to clear the back rail with more pace: The faster ground speed you have, the longer the distance the horse can travel when in the air over the fence. Compared to the vertical, your ideal takeoff distance is slightly closer to the base of the jump.

III.26 Triple bar: High Society III at the Morven Park Advanced Horse Trials.

• *Triple Bar* A triple bar is like an ascending oxer that has three or more rails—the

first rail being the lowest, with the others progressively getting taller to the back rail (fig. III.26). Due to its width, you must approach the jump on an even more open stride than you do for the oxer. It's also very important that you place your horse right at the base of the jump for takeoff. If you happen to get a longer-than-ideal distance, you're much more likely to take down the back rail with your horse's hind end.

• *Open Water* This will be the most "forward" you'll come to any jump. Again, the width can be significant, so it's important to place your horse close to the front rail (fig. III.27).

Cross-Country

• *Coffin or Sunken Road Combinations* The Coffin is one of the most talked about combinations (rail, ditch, rail). You often hear you need a "Coffin canter," which means a very powerful canter at a speed similar to what is seen in show jumping. You want this powerful canter to give your horse the best opportunity to be "quick" with his front end for the first element. A greener horse will begin

Cross-Country Simulation

In III.28 A you see the kinds of distractions Running Order faces while galloping on the cross-country course at the 2012 Rolex CCI****. At home, in the arena, one way we simulate the cross-country course is by using fake rocks, as shown in III.28 B and C. Often sold as well covers,

these rocks can get a horse's attention just like real terrain variations or unexpected distractions present themselves in competition. Not only do we place them under jumps, but in front of and behind them.

In the photos below we have two rocks set up on the landing of a vertical (rear and front views); I would plan to land between the two rocks. This placement often tempts a horse to peek at them when he's in the air. A greener horse is especially susceptible; often, he will not jump as well with his front end on takeoff, or he'll put down his hind end faster. He'll quickly learn to read a situation without compromising his jump form. This is critical to producing a safe and confident jumper.

III.29 Coffin jump: Crown Talisman going over the ditch, the second element of a Coffin jump at Pine Top Farm in Georgia.

to jump, but the moment he reaches the top of his jump he will notice the ditch a stride away (fig. III.29). He may then drop his legs and hit the jump. A horse without enough power may also be surprised and stop. You can't have enough power in a combination like this.

• *Galloping Fences and Steeplechase Fences* If you are an eventer you'll find that you get very good at these since they are the majority of the fences you'll encounter (figs. III.30 A & B). Jumping fences like this, you don't need to significantly slow your speed, but it is important to shift your horse's balance to make sure he is off his forehand and approaching with power. As you approach, roughly six strides out from the fence, open your hip angle and shift your weight slightly toward the rear. You'll be surprised how well your horse will respond to a slight

III.30 A & B Galloping fence: In A Running Order is going over a table out of a gallop at the Fork CIC***in North Carolina. Photo B shows a steeplechase-type fence: Crown Talisman at the 2012 Fair Hill International CCI** in Maryland.

III.31 Running Order jumping into the first water complex at the 2012 Rolex Kentucky CCI****.

shift in your balance and become further engaged. Your goal is to allow the jump itself to "back the horse off," rather than your hand.

• *Water Complex* Very much like the "coffin canter," you should have a lot of power for this, but not at a high rate of speed. This is especially critical with the larger drop fence and when the water level is deep: The deeper the water, the slower you need to jump into a water complex (fig. III.31).

• *Banks* "Up" banks should be approached with an active canter and an uphill balance (fig. III.32). You'll never be in trouble by adding too much leg at takeoff. It takes an extraordinary effort to jump to a higher ground level. Give the horse the support he needs. "Down" banks are a bit different. You should approach a down bank from a slow canter or trot. The most important

III.32 Running Order jumping out of the Sunken Road at the 2012 Rolex Kentucky CCI****.

Introducing Water

Here is Darby again. This time she is demonstrating how I like to introduce a young horse to water jumps (III.33 A–R).

To begin, I always try go do down a ramp into water alone, but if the horse stops, I quickly call in a friend for a lead (A & B).

While Jess and PJ lead us into the water, Darby wants to investigate further. I always let her drop her head to smell and get a closer look. I'll only add pressure with leg or whip if she begins to step backward (C).

This is a great photo! I'm just about to get wet, and doing my best not to fall off backward or grab her in the mouth in the process. Notice I am at the end of the reins at the buckle (D).

Once in the water, and on top of my horse, I'll let her hang out and sniff around more if she likes (E). I am always at the ready to push her forward should she decide that rolling is a good idea. In the past, I've made the mistake of giving a horse the benefit of the doubt and come away very wet as a result!

We are now trotting and cantering through alone (F–H).

After she is confident with the ramp in and out, I like to introduce the "up" bank. I'm doing my best to keep her straight and stay out of her way (I).

Again, I'm letting the reins slide so she can use her neck (J).

Knowing that she will probably "look" based on her reaction going down the ramp, I choose to get a lead from Jess and PJ down the bank into the water (K).

As she "looks," I'm sitting slightly back, giving her time and only adding leg when she starts to suck back (L).

Once we're in, we might as well jump out without anyone leading us (M & N).

Last but not least, we jump in and out alone (O–R).

thing to remember with a down bank is to give the horse enough time to process what is being asked. If you blindly run him at a bank, he'll literally canter off
into space. Give him time and the full use of his head and neck (figs. III.34 A–F).

• *Mounds and Steep Approaches*   Questions like these are becoming more and
more common. You will be surprised how quickly you'll lose energy and speed
as you go up a hill: You can lose 100 meters a minute with every step. Your plan
should be to get to the jump at the top of the mound with enough pace and
energy to jump it well. You cannot have too much energy at the base of the hill!

III.34 A–F Darby
and her first bank
experience: I'm
approaching with a
balanced pace and
giving her time and
freedom to fully check
out what is being
asked of her. I will only
apply pressure if she
sucks back.

III.35 A–D Photo A shows Crown Talisman at the 2012 Fair Hill International CCI** jumping an angled brush combination. Photo B is a corner coming out of the Sunken Road complex at the 2012 Rolex Kentucky CCI**** with Running Order. In C you see what we use daily at home to simulate the Triple Brush. With more experienced horses, we fill the gaps with actual brush. Your approach, jumping ideally, would be just left of the photographer.

Photo D was taken at the 2012 Rolex Kentucky CCI**** (a scalloped brush is commonly only seen at the 4* level—the high sides take away your ideal approach, forcing the horse and rider to jump straight and opening them up to run outs to either direction). What makes the Triple Brush even more challenging are the elements that precede it. In this case, you are looking at the third element: The first was an airy vertical, followed by one stride down a steep slope to a ditch, then a long three strides later was this Triple Brush. This requires extreme accuracy and a genuine partnership with your horse to navigate without trouble.

• *Corner, Angled, and Narrow Fences* Generally described as "accuracy questions," all of these fences should be approached with your hip angle slightly open, your center of gravity just behind your horse's, and a soft contact (figs. III.35 A–D). This places you in the best position possible to react to deviations on your approach and allow your horse to remain round and soft. The moment your horse becomes braced—oftentimes due to a stiff or harsh hand—he will begin to

wiggle, and a run-out is inevitable. You must steer with your legs rather than your hands for a successful jump!

Angled fences are the most basic example of an accuracy question you'll encounter in competition. They should be approached with caution, and where feasible and prudent, you should try to reduce the fence's angle by altering your approach. This will give your horse "one stride longer" to figure out what is being asked and will often allow him to jump the fence in better form.

There are two other main types of accuracy questions you'll encounter as you progress up the levels: The Corner and the Triple Brush (Chevron).

Of the two types, the Corner is the more forgiving. The horse approaches the Corner with fewer options—run out to the narrow side or jump it—whereas with the Triple Brush, the horse can run out to either side or stop. Corners are best jumped about one third the way in from the point

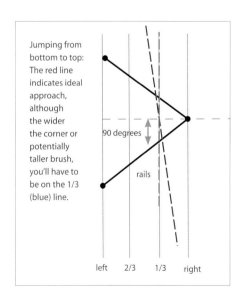

Jumping from bottom to top: The red line indicates ideal approach, although the wider the corner or potentially taller brush, you'll have to be on the 1/3 (blue) line.

90 degrees

rails

left   2/3   1/3   right

Diagram 6 Jumping the Corner.

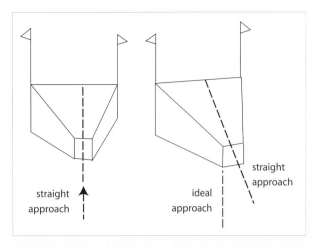

straight
approach

ideal
approach

straight
approach

Diagram 7
Jumping a Triple Brush/Chevron.

just about on the perpendicular of the bisected angle (Diagram 6). Triple Brushes are easiest to jump at a slight angle where one of the side faces can be used to make the jump appear wider than it is in actuality. If you were to draw a line extending from one of the sides, this should be the angle of your approach with your goal of placing your horse's feet at the inside edge of the front face of the jump (Diagram 7).

Both Corners and Triple Brushes can be simulated in an arena at home. Note that you should be able to jump them with quite a soft contact. If everything has to be absolutely perfect for your horse to jump these kinds of questions at home, you are bound for trouble in competition when distractions, design, and terrain are added to the equation.

tip *Walk your cross-country course with your warm-up in mind. Often you can simulate the turning or angled combinations in warm-up. This way, if your horse drifts (even the slightest bit), you have a chance to correct it prior to your cross-country start, and you'll head out of the box with great confidence, knowing you've already ridden part of the course!*

PART 3
How It Can Work for You, How It Has Worked for Me

· ▶

chapter seven

Strategies for Future Success

Minimize Your Training Aids

"Reduction" or "simplification" is your "solution." Less is more when it comes to riding and training horses. All too often, people will overcomplicate a situation using every gadget in the world to fix all of their problems. But, the issues do not lie in the equipment used, they lie in the horse's previous training. The same holds true for the aids you use: Every day, your goal should be to refine and reduce the use of your aids so that your horse can become more sensitive and responsive. You shouldn't finish your ride out of breath and sore. What should you do when an old problem rears its ugly head? "Fixing" a problem is not a final solution. You can seldom completely resolve an issue. The beauty of playing a role in your horse's progress is that you'll be aware of all the steps taken along the way. If he happens to try to resort to some of his old tricks, you'll know how to correct him quickly.

As you train, you'll inevitably reach a few forks in the road. It is your job to identify when the horse goes the wrong way—even the slightest bit—and get him back on track. Remember, in order to progress further, you have to push the envelope, and inevitably, as you ask for more, you will encounter resistance. However, bear in mind the resistance you encounter when teaching a new skill should not be viewed as disobedience, since most likely it is a genuine misunderstanding of what is being asked.

When you hit one of these bumps in the road, rather than getting "wrapped up" in the situation, take a step back and break down the exercise at hand. Everything you ask of a horse can be further broken down, so make the desired result become your horse's idea! The best horsemen in the world consistently produce horses that enjoy their job and appear to perform anything asked as if they had thought of doing it. Keep this idea in your head while training.

Applying My Philosophy to Other Problems

While this book has covered a large number of the problems encountered while riding and training horses, in no way can I touch on every instance and every issue. However, I hope it is giving you a basic framework to extrapolate beyond. Horses will always keep you on your toes. Like any skill, you are best able to handle issues when the solution becomes second nature to you. An instinctive response will be infinitely quicker than anything you have to contemplate.

As you progress as a rider, it never hurts to get on as many horses as you can manage. To get better at riding "difficult" horses you have to ride difficult horses. Keep in mind that when you stop learning you will stop progressing.

In training, horses generally go down the easier path, though, of course, there are exceptions. Some horses, by nature, are prone to rearing and others are buckers or become barn sour. If your horse is one of these, study the problem. Go at it with a vengeance! I strongly recommend twisting a friend's arm to come out not only to watch but to video you riding your horse in a situation where the problem is likely to present itself. This is assuming you're not placing yourself in undue harm in the process, but as I've said before, video is about the most useful tool I've ever come across to help me figure out my horses' tendencies.

Strategies for
Future Success

As with all challenges, the more heads you have working on the problem, the better. Invite the best horsemen around—trainers and riders—for pizza and beer and watch your video one evening. This is a difficult and uncomfortable process for some people, but it will ultimately yield the best results. If possible, find a television large enough that has the technology to play your video in slow motion. Look for subtle clues before the horse's bad behavior occurs. Nine times out of ten you'll be able to identify a few key behaviors on your horse's part that signal when he's about to "strike." If you have video of the particular problem occurring at different times, you are even better off.

For example, you can take your barn-sour horse out toward the ring and have the problem occur. Then, head back to the barn, turn around and attempt to go out again. If possible, get the second video shot from a different angle. It will astound you what can be learned from just 20 seconds. This barn-sour horse may "pop" his shoulder just before dropping behind your leg again, before he grabs the bit to pull the 180-degree spin back to his friends. When you can interrupt that process, stopping the shoulder first, you may have the key to the problem right there at hand. Be open to suggestions without becoming defensive: This is a most difficult thing for someone going through a tough time, but defensiveness is a big roadblock to progress.

> **tip** *Technology is available to video your ride on your iPhone, iPad, and Android devices. The USET uses a very reasonably priced app called Dartfish, but there are plenty of other options that video your jumping or dressage that can then be played back in slow motion, reverse, and forward— all just by using a scrolling wheel at the bottom of the screen.*

When and How to Raise Your Expectations

When do you push the boundaries or your comfort level (because there always comes a point when you will have a good grasp of what is asked at your current level of training)? The rule of thumb I live by regardless of discipline is as follows: When I find I'm bored at a certain level and can consistently produce good results regardless of conditions, it's time to move up. Simply speaking, there will always be a learning curve, for both you and your horse, with any new skill set. And, as with any sport, you will be constantly checking back and improving your basics—they are the foundation of all skills.

PART 3: HOW IT CAN WORK FOR YOU, HOW IT HAS WORKED FOR ME **189**

Even when you feel that you're not the world's best, it doesn't mean you are not ready to move further forward. You need to feel comfortable with what's being asked, be familiar with the aids being used, feel confident applying them, and know the potential downsides of using too much of one or another independent aid. It's the combination of aids that's going to produce a movement—at whatever level of training.

The best example here is a half-pass, a movement that is introduced in Third Level dressage and at Advanced Level in eventing. In order to produce this sideways and forward movement, your horse bends around your inside leg going in the direction of travel. The sequence of aids is: a slight weight shift to the inside; the outside leg slightly back; the inside leg at the girth along with the inside rein controls the amount of bend; and the outside rein and leg, along with your weight, creates the lateral motion.

While this can seem quite complicated at first, it becomes more and more natural as your riding progresses. Breaking the sequence down, you need to know that if you use too much outside leg you risk pushing the haunches ahead of the shoulders, lose the inside bend, and lose the connection from the hindquarters to the bit. Each component must be analyzed so when you're heading across the ring and your ground person says "haunches trailing" you know to add your outside leg and a bit of outside rein.

This will not come overnight. Break things down and slow them down. In this example, start at the walk, and have a trainer who is intimately familiar with dressage assessing you and answering any questions you may have. (This same process should be applied to all aspects of your riding.)

Once you can execute the movement—not perfectly, but well—it's time to start looking to add to your horse's repertoire. You'll find that the more you ask of him, the easier all aspects of your riding will become.

Do keep in mind, things have to happen easily. When you have to work incredibly hard to get a mediocre effort, don't continue to push. Always be willing to take that step back for two steps forward. *Pushing* through will inevitably result in your horse flying backward in his training—faster than you can blink.

I've found one of the best ways to raise expectations and refine skills is through observation. It's very easy to think that you are as far along as you possibly can be for a horse of the age and experience that your horse is at this moment in time, but try to find a national- or international-level competition in your area, and watch the best of the best. Often, it's most interesting to watch the best riders on their greenest horses. You will soon pick up on the little elements that allow them to progress and build confidence in their partners quicker than you'd expect possible. The great thing about this is that you will be able to go home and implement some of the nuances you see at the show grounds. If there isn't a show nearby, do a quick search on YouTube: There are plenty of young-horse competitions online. I assure you, you'll learn something by watching, and the best part about it is that there's no limit, and it's free!

Conclusion

Your life with horses will be full of its ups and downs. Enjoy the good times and keep them stored away in your mind for the bad times. You have to be resilient and unemotional. Your ultimate goal as a trainer is to present options to your horse in such a way that he chooses the one that also happens to be the one you desire.

Throughout your time with horses, do your best to stay positive. When communicating, avoid the common traps, for example: Don't pull, don't drift, don't go slowly. Instead, visualize and act on what you want. Think: *Go forward, bend left, rebalance*. Ask and allow. You'll be surprised how well visualization will guide you and your horse forward. Remember, no nagging!

Everyone's goals are different with horses, but what unites all disciplines is the desire of a rider to have a confident partner who enjoys his job. Just like people, horses need variety in their job in order to keep things fresh and their motivation level high. Don't get stuck in the ring preparing for the next big show or outing, day in and day out. It always amazes me how much just one fun day out on the trail per week can help improve competition results.

Overtraining or drilling your horse will take a significant mental and physical toll—on both of you. Break your daily goals down into manageable bits of information, systematically approach and achieve them, then go out for a hack!

chapter eight

Real Case Studies:
Horses I Have Ridden

L et's start with a little background before heading into specific stories. I love figuring each horse out. I have always prided myself at being able to get on a horse, quickly come up with an accurate assessment of his problems, and get going on the solutions in minutes.

The first day a horse arrives, I'm always excited to hop on and get a feel for him. I've learned that it's always best to get an idea of what to expect before putting your foot in the stirrup, so with a new one, I try to get the basic information: age, breed, background (levels he's competed at, results) and as much as possible about the problem at hand. In addition, I also like to find out what strategies have been tried in the past to fix the horse's issue and if there were any side effects. For instance, his rider might tell me that he's barn sour and doesn't want to leave his friends. Upon further questioning, I find out that after he's stopped moving forward, the rider can only seem to get him to turn left but when she tries to turn right, he rears. At this point, I have a very good idea of what to expect although I usually also follow up asking how high he goes when he rears, always keeping in mind that it's not worth seriously hurting myself over a horse. (When his rider says that he flips over, I'll recommend the horse be moved down the road to someone else—remember my "learning experience" on p. 95?)

As for the problems themselves, I've also learned that it's very important to consider the source of the information. You have to be as good at reading the owners and riders as you do the horses. It's a human trait that some people exaggerate the degree in which their horse's behavior has taken over their life, while others will be very accurate, even understate the problem. After riding countless "problem" horses, at times it's easy to start getting overconfident. The wonderful thing about horse sports is that you won't remain that way for long. Once or twice, I've had an owner drop a horse off and say, "He can seriously buck." Of course he does...I'm thinking to myself; I've ridden thousands of buckers in the past and haven't been seriously sent into orbit yet. Well, two minutes later, I've promptly found myself in the sand looking up at my new project.

The Alchemyst

The Alchemyst, known around the barn as "Albert," came to me with a list of issues. He had been bred to event up in Canada, and was purchased as a prospect by the Blackmans. He was a medium-built Canadian Thoroughbred gelding. I'm not sure I've ridden a horse with a proportionally shorter neck. Like most seriously athletic horses, he was sharp as a tack. This intelligence worked to my advantage once he was fighting on my side, but like most horses in this situation, convincing him that *my* plans should be *his* plans was the challenge!

He had been eventing for a year or so, and had gone unsuccessfully through Preliminary Level. He also had a reputation of jumping out of fields; I knew from Day One that I should be careful with him. The more athletic the horse is, the more challenging the fix will be, and the more dangerous it can be for the rider.

Al had been to a number of very skilled riders in his past, though I wouldn't say that any of these created his issues. But, at the same time, I was given the task of trying to unravel the roots of his behavior and see if I could get him straightened out. He was an excellent jumper, very brave, and very quick.

Albert came to the farm, and I hopped on. I had been told just a few minutes earlier that he would just shut down and not go any farther. The previous riders had tried to get after him with the whip with no lasting luck—they hadn't made a whole lot of progress and wanted to see what I could do with him.

My first thoughts were that he may have been overfaced, or he just didn't completely understand what was being asked. He didn't seem like a malicious horse on my first impression. (Your first impression is usually right.)

So I got on and instantly knew what they were describing. Not only did his neck feel as if it was 2 inches long, but he also was very reluctant to go forward. Not that he wasn't listening to my leg, but it almost felt as if he didn't think he was allowed to go forward. A horse like this can be tricky because you have to make him believe that "forward" is always an option. You have to be very careful with your contact and never restrict him from going forward. At the same time, you do have to teach him to confidently take the contact from you. Riding around on a looped rein is not the answer.

He had a few good tricks up his sleeve. You could be at any gait and this horse would plant his front feet and spin the other way faster than I imagined possible. I can't understate how much this problem was compounded due to the short neck—if I was at all forward in my position, I was toast!

The funniest, well nerve-racking, example of this was in the warm-up of Stuart Horse Trials in Victor, New York. Stuart, for those who've not attended, is a very well-run horse trial with a "big time" feel. It has all sorts of tents, vendors, banners—all of which are beautiful, but they were terrifying in Albert's mind. The walk to the dressage ring from stabling is always a challenge, in that it's not close, and the path leads you directly through the center of the cross-country. I managed to survive the first few days without too much trouble. Although not performing a winning dressage test, he was well composed. I figured we might be getting somewhere.

Cross-country was next up. We entered warm-up and that short neck was showing its "ugly head." It just happens to put you on edge: He could "ball" himself up quicker than you could blink. With a horse like this, it's usually best to do a slow progressive warm-up. Very much like cold-backed horses, you just have to allow them to figure out that they can let go of the tension (see p. 106). Some resistance to forward motion can be tolerated, but every time it happens and the horse tenses up, I try to go right into a leg-yield or simply change direction and bend. As soon as possible, I'll work into the canter. The opportune time is nothing you can pinpoint; I'd be trotting along going freely forward, start to ask for the canter, and he'd instantly contract every muscle in his thorax. Back to the trot we'd go, checking back in with the canter in a few minutes. We got into the canter and loosened everything up.

I felt confident that we were good to start jumping. Little did I know approaching the first jump how wrong I was! Just imagine, finally he feels pretty loose. Heading to the first cross-rail at a canter, I see a good distance. He takes off with no trouble at all. He landed without issue, however, that's where we stopped. Literally! He took off and landed after the jump in a *halt*. I've only had one other horse that I think might be able to accomplish this—if he wanted to. I was astounded how strong this horse was naturally and how athletic he was to be able to land "planted."

While he was composed about it, I didn't get that memo. Remember that short neck I spoke of earlier? Not that it was a long way to go, but I was instantly sitting on his ears. Thankfully, he was one to usually stick his head up higher; had he kept it level or lowered it, I'd have been sliding down the neck landing on my butt in front of him.

You don't have a whole lot of time to react here. I knew how quickly this horse could spin. I had to shimmy down from his ears to the security of the saddle. The one and only time I was thankful of his ungodly short neck! It didn't take long, and I was back in the saddle—certainly in shock, but back on top. I was ready to fight another day, or in this case attempt to get him landing—but *not* halting—on the other side of the fence. It doesn't help your time on course when you're halting after each jump.

I got him moving again, and reapproached the same jump. This time, I was sitting back as if I were jumping into the leaf pit at Morven Park. A little ridiculous, I know, seeing that the jump was 18 inches tall and we were minutes away from riding a Preliminary cross-country round. I had to figure something out quickly to get this resolved. He wasn't one that you could just smack on landing. It would actually have the opposite effect; he already felt confined, as if he wasn't allowed to go forward. I was able to jump this same jump on a circle, where as soon as we took off I could start turning him. This had been the key to resolving the shutting down months earlier on the flat, so I figured it was my best shot here. It worked like a charm. Just like a cold-backed horse that takes a deep breath and acts as if nothing ever happened, he relaxed and from that point forward, he jumped like a normal horse.

He finished up very well at Stuart. Consulting with his owners, we decided that the goal would be to head to the Morven Park CCI* that fall. He continually improved over the months leading up to Morven. He was a great cross-country horse, really everything you could want—very quick on his feet and mentally aware beyond his years. The flatwork was always the most difficult for him: He'd still get tight in his core at times. This also started a chain reaction that further shortened his neck; unfortunately, judges don't look highly on this conformational trait.

During the weeks leading up to Morven, I was feeling confident that Albert had a reasonably good shot at putting in a solid performance. This event was still held in the "classic" eventing format, and it was always an unknown how a horse was going to handle the steeplechase and roads and tracks phases—all of which were performed before exiting the start box on cross-country.

The competition arrived. His dressage score put him at a respectable position—I can't remember off the top of my head where, but in the Top Ten or so. Endurance day worked well for us: Phase A (roads and tracks) did a good job of getting the hump out of his back; steeplechase, as always, was a blast— he always had a good gallop and was no worse for the wear by the time we reached the cross-country phase.

The course was nearly flawless. I did have one brief scare toward the end where we had a rollback turn to a downhill vertical. I knew this would be difficult for him because tight turns still had the potential to shut him down—especially in this case because it was turning away from the start and his friends. I didn't ride the line as well as I should, and to make matters worse, I managed to lose his shoulder to the outside. I spoke earlier about having a light contact while approaching a jump where the horse is "drawing" you forward to it (see p. 149): Well I had that feeling about 10 strides out, but then the turn happened, I lost the shoulder, he was over-bent, and about four strides from the fence, "spitting the bit" or backing off. Not a good feeling! Just in time I was able to get him straightened out and due to his sheer athleticism, we jumped the vertical in good form. We finished up inside the time allowed—no small feat.

He trotted up well the next morning, so we were on to show jumping. He felt great warming up. It always amazes me how the longer cross-country course can have a very positive effect on horses. He jumped well and moved up to finish fourth.

Following the CCI* he had a few weeks off as is customary. Early that winter the Blackmans and I decided sell him. I couldn't have asked for a better rider to come forward to take over the ride. Debbie Rosen bought him and continued on with his training. She's done a wonderful job with him, although she's told me that with Albert she's ended up on the ground more often than she likes to admit. At this point, he's successfully been around a number of CCI*** events and has been to the Rolex CCI**** twice.

This is probably one of the most rewarding aspects of working with horses: to see a horse whose path was unclear—if not headed in the wrong direction—do an about-face and have such success in his life.

Crown Talisman

"Tali" is the second and only horse that has the core strength to allow him to land "halted" as Albert did at Stuart Horse Trials. I would go as far to say that Tali is even stronger and more impressive in his natural body awareness and strength. He stands 17.1 hands tall and is a striking, dark bay Thoroughbred-Holsteiner cross gelding. He is just about the perfect physical specimen and the most talented horse I've ever had the pleasure of riding in dressage. Not only is he good there, but he's an exceptionally good, brave jumper as well.

Tali was a homebred of Martha Thomas, who along with Babsi Clark, has brought up some exceptionally talented horses for me to ride and train. He arrived basically green-broke. He initially had been started as a three-year-old and was very quiet and frankly, easy. However, when he was five, and he arrived at my place, he was anything *but* easy. In the past he had been ridden at walk, trot, and canter. Martha and Babsi warned me against just getting on him from the start.

I got out the longe line with Tali and as I watched him trot around me, they told me that they believed he'd make a good eventer and wanted to see if they could sell him. They were going to leave him with me for a month to see what I thought. He certainly looked the part, but the trot was nothing terribly special. However, the moment he picked up the canter, I was hooked on this horse. In addition, he didn't have a malicious bone in his body, even if he was a bit of a rogue.

I managed to get on with some help. The first day I just walked and picked up the trot for a short while. I knew from longeing him and from what I'd been told that he was athletic, but someone can tell you that all day long and it just doesn't seem to sink in until you experience it firsthand. My introduction to Tali came in the form of noise: I'm still not sure what it was but some loud sharp bang in the background sent us into the air. Unlike any horse I've ever ridden, he could "levitate" himself on a whim. Not a buck or rear, just all four feet off the ground at once, without warning. It took me a while to understand what was happening.

As I mentioned earlier, horses are creatures of habit. Most behaviors will repeat themselves. It didn't really dawn on me exactly what was happening until we were at his first event in Aiken, South Carolina, that spring. If he heard a loud noise or bang, regardless of the gait, he'd levitate and spin so that upon landing, he would be facing the direction of the noise, planted like a statue, with his ears pricked to figure out where exactly it came from. I can't find the words to describe how strong he was and how it's possible to be trotting along, then in the air doing a 180-degree turn, then landing absolutely still. All other horses would be struggling for balance, or take a few steps to get planted into the ground—not Tali.

His reactivity to sound was clear the first day, but by Day Two the story started to unravel further. He had another equally impressive and difficult-to-stay-on trick. After longeing, I led him up to the mounting block and hopped on. Faster than I imagined possible, we were in full reverse and accelerating closer and closer to the back wall of the indoor. I was thinking to myself, "this is bad." I didn't think he had noticed the kick board, and figured I only had a few more seconds before the inevitable impact. To my disbelief, it didn't happen.

Again, I found myself equally in shock when he reared up, and not just any rear. After reaching maximum height, you usually have a moment before the front feet return to earth. I soon realized I had much more than that, and was thinking I very well might end up in the rafters, when he suddenly "bucked out" of the rear. I would almost describe it as a jump of an imaginary fence with a serious kick at the top. Once his feet did hit the ground, with me still attached, we bolted forward. Just one hell of a ride!

I figured I was in good shape once he started to bolt: I could at least control the direction, and we were going forward. I was able to turn him and on a circle we went. I got him to the walk and I picked my stirrups back up. From that point forward, he really wasn't much different from the day before. Unfortunately, this full-reverse-rear-buck-then-bolt trick didn't go away quickly. To this day I'm still most nervous getting on him, but we've come to an understanding. I make sure the girth is tight and allow him to walk forward.

How did we get to this point? Well, he couldn't run backward if I had him turning. This whole process took weeks, but I would get on and quickly open the outside rein to turn him right. If he stepped back, the wall was soon there to help me out. Every day I would get on and off countless times, until his behavior was not perfect, but at least predictable.

After the first month, I had two local professionals come out to see him; both passed on him instantly. Not only was mounting an issue, but his trot was slow to improve: It was quite tense and choppy, and at times he almost looked lame. He had no physical issues, but the overall tension made a bigger trot impossible. Long story short, he was going to be a tough sell. I couldn't sell him to an amateur because I was afraid she would get hurt just trying to get on him, and I couldn't sell him to a professional because he was not proven and didn't trot well enough. He had the talent to go into dressage or eventing, but in both cases, the standard today is so high that you ideally want to start with an excellent, clean-moving horse. Tali was not that.

I spoke to Martha about the problem. She agreed that it would be difficult, and after discussing it further, she offered me a barter arrangement where I could assume ownership in exchange for training another horse of theirs for five months. Funnily enough, about a week earlier, he was fully tacked up in the aisle of the barn. I reached over to grab a drink and wasn't holding onto the reins. He promptly bolted out. (Had this not happened, I don't think I would have taken the chance on him because I wouldn't have seen the potential in his trot.)

It was amazing to watch this horse that usually shuffled around the ring, floating across the ground from field to field saying hello to every friend on the property. I actually found myself, holding a bucket of grain still, rather than shaking it to get Tali's attention in the hope of catching him. Instead, I just stood and watched. This doesn't happen often, but it was just cool to see him move.

I thought to myself at that moment that somehow I needed to keep this horse and to figure out how to unlock that potential.

It took me nearly a year before he went from his mediocre trot to a world-beating gait. In all my years of riding, I've seen slow and measured progress in horses. Sure, on occasion, a "light bulb" blinks on, but this was like turning on the football stadium lights—illuminating the ring like daylight! The first year had passed; Tali had been doing well. He'd usually score in the mid to high 30s. He had progressed from Beginner Novice to finish up the year with a few events at Training Level.

I was working to improve his trot lengthenings to prepare for the move up to Preliminary Level the following spring. It's not a complicated exercise, but I was asking him to lengthen for a few strides and to compress. This process was repeated a number of times, and then it happened: the most amazing experience of my life with horses. I asked him to collect after a lengthening and he went into this explosive, animated passage. I nearly fell off for two reasons: First, the shock of what was happening, and second, due to his suspension in the trot. That first day, I was able to keep that suspension when going to the right. The next day, I could get it going both right and left. I couldn't hold it for long, but it was there. From that point on, I knew I was riding a world-beater.

That spring, he moved up to Preliminary. I couldn't hold the trot for an entire test; for that matter, I often couldn't hold it for entire movements. Our scores that spring varied dramatically. If I could hold the suspension for most of the test, our score was in the 20s; if I couldn't, we were in the upper 30s. The lack of a consistent rhythm took us down in the short term.

This same spring, Larry and Amelia Ross entered into a partnership with me to secure Tali's future with us. As we all know, horses are extremely expensive, and without their help, I'm not sure I'd still have him. I'm very fortunate to have such ardent supporters.

That spring continued with more and more consistency in his dressage. The scores improved likewise. He finished up 2010 winning six events, the American Eventing Championships, and was in second place for Preliminary Horse of the Year with the USEA. He has continued to progress very well, moving up to the Advanced and CCI*** Level. In 2012 he was named to the USEF's National Training List. He continued his successful ways in 2013, finishing fourth at the

Fair Hill International CCI*** and tied for third for the Pro Tour Leaderboard. Aside from his eventing career, I plan to continue his training in dressage. I fully expect that some day in the future, he'll be competing at the FEI levels of dressage, as well!

Valant

Valant, known around the barn as Lenny, was a 16.3-hand, solidly built, Holsteiner Warmblood gelding who was bred to jump. Many of his siblings have been competitive at Grand Prix level, so I figured he had a good chance to join them. From the first moment I jumped him I knew Lenny would make it.

At that point, my "bread and butter" business was short-term rehab of "difficult" horses. For a few years, we'd had horses coming in for one to three months on average, 12 to 15 of them at a time. I had heard just about everything from owners and had become a little jaded with the whole explanation-of-the-problem process. A horse would come in, the owner would tell me he bucked or reared worse than she's seen in the past. Most times, it was not an issue. I could have the horse back on the straight and narrow in a week or so. From that point, I'd start training him further so that the owner wouldn't have a problem maintaining the fix.

Every once in a while, we'd get a "boomerang": a horse that would come in, get fixed, and return home, but then be back with the same problem again just a few months later. I figured Lenny was going to fall into that category. His owner, Carl Hartman, told me he was a big baby who appeared a little "dead" but was explosive. He'd had a number of local professionals near his hometown ride him; nearly all had fallen off him. Worse yet, in the process of falling off, they scared Lenny more.

Carl pulled in with a nondescript truck and trailer. A few minutes later, Lenny bolted off the trailer looking like a stag that had been shot at! He was an impressive horse, that was not in question. We tacked him up and headed down to the arena. Despite Carl's warnings, I figured I could just hop on and get to work.

Apparently, Lenny's spook was the biggest issue. After getting on, I soon found out what Carl had been talking about. First off, I'm very familiar with tall, athletic horses. At my height (6 foot 3 inches) most of the horses I've managed to pick out are 16.3 hands, or taller. Lenny was all of that, but more solid than anything I had at the farm. I picked up a trot and started around the ring.

He was just little more than green broke at this point, though he did walk, trot, canter and jump small cross-rails. My first indication of his power and quickness occurred as I passed a plastic barrel. As often happens, some sand was kicked up and hit the barrel, making a noise. Before I could process what had happened, we were roughly 10 feet to my left. I was—shockingly—still on, but astounded. I realized that it was in my interest to pay closer attention to Carl's advice; if I didn't, I was going to be lying in pain on the ground!

Before returning home, Carl wanted to see me jump a small fence. Afterward, I was told it was to see if I could stay on the horse! I approached the jump, expecting a big jump. I figured if the "spook" was a precursor that this jump might be something special. I was not wrong—we just about jumped the standards! Still to this day, I have not jumped any horse with the power or quickness of Lenny. It's a sensation that I'll never forget: You are literally just shot up in the air.

A year or so later, I had hit the dirt a number of times coming off him. There was the first show where a local trainer scared the pants off him by yelling at her student. He was sensitive, as I have mentioned, and every time she screamed, Lenny would jump—one of the many times he got me with an "added-spin" trick.

There was another time I called Carl after being clean bucked off. I was both excited I wasn't hurt but also just in awe of this horse's power. I was in a dressage saddle, cantering on a circle, spiraling in. I reached about 10 meters in size, and I think it must have been one of the first times Lenny realized how to compress his body and what power that afforded him. He bucked, and literally before I knew it, I had done a full flip, landing on my butt on the ground in front of him facing in the direction we were heading. I'm usually pretty good at sticking on "bucks," but not this one. He coiled up and I didn't stand a chance.

Another once-in-a-lifetime occurrence happened just a few months later. At this point, Lenny was jumping around 4 feet or so. I had set up a vertical that may have been a bit bigger than the rest of the fences jumped that day and also added a Liverpool under it. As I said, Lenny was a spooky horse: I should have started with a nice, long, straight approach. But that's no fun! So, I jumped it for the first time off a rollback turn. I don't think he saw the jump until we were a stride out or so. He then had the biggest kick off the ground I'd ever felt from a horse, and at the same time, he added a little twist so as to not touch the rail. I soon found myself flying next to him, 8 feet in the air. I can still remember being on the right side of him, about the same height as his neck, just separated by 2 feet or so off to the side. The landing was not all that much fun—it's a long way to fall. Again, I found myself in the sand just thinking to myself how incredible this horse is, how I never imagined any animal could have that much power. I have not been "jumped off" a horse since and don't expect it will happen again. I have to admit, if it *were* to happen again, I would like to think I'd enjoy it just as much the second time around!

I learned a lot of things other than countless ways to fall off riding Lenny. He started in the "itty bitty" jumpers and progressed over the next two years all the way up to his first Grand Prix—and mine, too. His "twitchiness" never has gone away; it started to diminish but at the same time, that is what makes him an excellent jumper. You have to keep in mind that through all of your training, you're looking to fill the gaps in your horse's education. Try to make him better, but at the same time, do not destroy his personality. Individual quirks will, in most cases, work for you. Great horses are not "dead heads," and they are not easy. Embrace and enjoy them for what they are—individuals.

Running Order

Last, but not least, was Running Order, my "horse of a lifetime." He is a tall, lanky, 17.1-hand, Irish-bred Thoroughbred gelding. When he came to me, he was owned by Patti Springsteen and had started his life racing in Ireland. He was originally trained by the world-renowned jockey, now trainer, Enda Bolger. Running Order was bred as a cross-country racehorse. In Ireland and across Europe, cross-country racing is quite popular. It is very much like steeplechase racing in the United States, with the addition of banks, ditches, and hedges. Enda said that Running Order didn't have a top gear: He was good to finish in the middle of the pack, and never really had the drive to win.

Following his racing career he took a flight over to the States to his new home with the Springsteens. He was briefly at their New Jersey farm before heading south to another barn for the winter of show jumping in Wellington, Florida. He was less than successful in the show ring. He is a typical "Irishman": very smart, athletic, and quirky. He's also very spooky, more so than you'd ever imagine an Advanced Level event horse to be. Down in Florida, he was bucking, rearing, and reluctant to leave the barn. He just wasn't fitting in with the rest of the horses there, and Patti received a call asking her to take Running Order back—he just wasn't working out. Luckily, I had taught Patti's then sister-in-law, Jennifer, in a few clinics. Jennifer had a promising young eventer herself. After they spoke, it was decided that Running Order should come to visit my place.

He got off the trailer in April 2008 and was exactly as described: a very lanky, gangly, six-year-old. He came along with another horse, and one of them was to be sold. From the first time I got on Running Order, I knew he had to stay. As with most jumping horses I had to see how well he jumped on the first day. After warming up, I set up a cavalletti to canter over. It couldn't have been more than one foot tall. As I approached the fence he was "back-pedaling." I figured he'd never seen one before. I was shocked when he took off at the base of the jump. He was about 4 feet in the air, with his knees up by his eyes. I knew he was a big-time horse then and there. Horses just don't jump like that very often. He was just oozing with talent.

Every horse is different, that goes without saying, but he was a freak. He figured things out faster than any horse I'd worked with. There were a few very strange aspects of his progression. The first, I've already mentioned: He was very spooky. But, he was careful and hardly ever put a foot wrong.

The second oddity did not really show itself until he reached Training Level that fall. At Training, the horses start to see larger Trakehners, which are jumps consisting of a log over a ditch. These are usually built in a tree line or in the middle of a field. Jumped at speed, you don't really have to spend that much time setting up for one; confident horses jump them without blinking. The peculiar thing about Running Order is that every time I reached a Trakehner or an open ditch, he'd be sucking back getting behind my leg from eight strides out. I couldn't figure out what was happening, seeing that he'd schooled as many of these jumps as any other of my horses. He was far more unsure about them than any horse I'd ridden to that point.

He never felt as if he was going to stop, but as the fences got bigger I needed to carry more pace than he wanted to in order to make easy work of them. The sure way to get a Trakehner "problem" is to "climb over" one, or worse yet, land in one. It didn't make sense until I spent a week at Enda's place. The first time I went out cross-country riding him, I was shocked. We went out of the farm, and within two minutes we crossed two of what I thought were massive ditches. I soon found out these were just a small taste of what was to come.

All the stories you hear about Irish hunting are true. No wonder they are such great cross-country riders. From Day One, they are hanging on for dear life over terrain that most riders in the United States would say was impossible to jump. Suddenly, Running Order's ditch behavior made all the sense in the world. We'd be at a full gallop across a field and reach the edge, which of course was next to a ditch, wire fence, hedge, or combination of all three. Every ditch we got to was jumped from a walk. A lot of them had a wire fence on the back side, or if it was a double ditch, you'd jump the first onto a mound with a wire fence and then traverse down the mound until there was an opening in the fence in order to jump the second ditch. So with me, he'd been sucking back at the ditches in order to figure out what was being asked and whether there was something on the back side to be aware of. I'm sure he was thinking I was a crazy idiot—running blindly at a ditch with no regard of what was on the other side!

He is still one of the best jumping horses I've ever ridden. His cat-like instincts were honed from countless rides growing up in Ireland. Just after the horses are broken over there they are out of the ring and into the "country." It's an eye-opening experience, and one trip every rider should do at least once in her life. You'll be amazed at what horses at a young age are capable of accomplishing. Many people are too cautious with their young horses. Within reason, drop them into the "pool." They will sink or swim. Take the swimmer.

Running Order finished off his first year at Training Level. He's a weird case in that he'd actually had a lot of jumping experience in Ireland but very little formal training on the flat. So his biggest obstacle was the dressage phase. We also needed to keep him challenged (and learning) with the jumping. Following that first winter concentrating on the dressage, he started at Preliminary Level. He finished up that spring with a win at the Virginia CCI* held in the classic eventing format. This format, with roads and tracks and steeplechase phases, suited him to a tee. He has an enormous, economical gallop that covers the ground with ease. Following a short break, he moved up to Intermediate and finished off the year at the Fair Hill CCI**. This was one of the proudest moments of my riding life.

The weather that weekend was horrendous. Following dressage, he was sitting in eighth—not a bad spot to be, but then the rain came, and just continued. The temperature dropped and the rain became harder. In the morning, the event personnel made some modifications to the cross-country course. I was actually unable to walk out to see these in person because I was the fourth horse to go out. Communication was poor and we were in the barn, tacked up and just waiting for the cue to get on. Anyone who's been to the Fall CCI at Fair Hill knows that the barn is roughly a half-mile from the cross-country warm up. I walked out of the stable area and down the long tree line to the warm-up area. It was a surreal situation: As far as I could see ahead and behind me, there was… well…nothing. No people, no horses, just the unrelenting cold rain. I reached the warm-up and there were a few volunteers waiting for the day to start. I asked if we were a "go" to start on time. They affirmed we were good to go, but there were still no other riders to be seen. Anyway. I warmed up, and was just about to head to the start box when I saw the first other rider.

I knew these conditions would be perfect for us, well, maybe not perfect, but better for us than for nearly anyone else. Running Order had grown up running in mud like this, so I went out on the course to see what could be done. He jumped around better than I could have ever expected; in the end, the weather worked in our favor. Wet conditions always restrict your ability to micromanage your jumping. You really just have to ride forward and not touch the reins. Running Order is best with that sort of riding, anyway. We finished up with just a few time penalties, but went clean. We had Running Order completely cooled out by the time the next rider reached the finish line: the next few riders that started after us had problems across the board. We finished up the day in fourth position.

In the show jumping phase the next day we had one rail down due to his spookiness: There was a combination along the rail and Running Order decided to shy at a photographer standing right there rather than pay attention to the jump. Such is life; second at his first CCI** wasn't a bad result!

He then moved up to Advanced the following spring and was a member of the Developing Rider Tour to Boekelo, Holland, that fall. He then added a third place at the Jersey Fresh CCI***, and a sixth at the Fair Hill CCI*** to finish up 2011.

The winter and spring of 2012 were spent refining the "raw product." At this point, Running Order had spent a year and a half at the Advanced Level. The Rolex Kentucky was in our sights. The USET has an exceptional training program that runs through the winter and spring months. The training sessions were different this time around; we spent a lot of time trying to iron out the small kinks that could limit our chances at an international medal.

Specifically, we worked very hard on increasing his lateral suppleness to allow him to increase the level of engagement and pushing power. Along with this work on the flat, we focused on the same traits while jumping. From Day One he was a difficult horse to adjust while maintaining an appropriate level of energy.

Running Order continued to get stronger and more confident with each day. We had a great series of competitions leading up to Kentucky. Dressage day rolled around and, while not flawless, he put in an excellent performance. He was sitting just outside of the Top Ten in a very solid field. As a 10-year-old, he was also one of the youngest in the competition.

Cross-country day was a nerve-racking one, to say the least. The first handful of competitors out on course were not making it look easy! By the time I hopped on, there had been a few combinations clean across the finish line. Luckily, I knew I was sitting on an exceptionally talented horse. The course rode well throughout. I did have a run out at the Coffin combination: It was a difficult complex where the first jump was a hanging log, then one stride over a ditch and about three-and-a-half strides to a narrow brush. I was a little slow to respond after a large jump over the ditch. Running Order never had a chance to see the third element—until it was too late. I was very proud of him: He continued on and made easy work of the remainder of the course.

Show jumping on the third day was another story! He felt as if he'd had the previous day off, rather than running around an eleven-and-a-quarter minute minute cross-country course. He was back to his spooky ways. I had to ride the first fence as if it was the scariest he'd seen in his life! We finished up very well: eighteenth in our first four star. (I have a narrated helmet-cam video of this ride posted on YouTube and my website dpequestrian.com. It's unlike anything you have ever seen!)

Despite my best efforts to purchase Running Order, he was sold by the Springsteens in the summer of 2012. Although a terribly difficult pill to swallow, if he couldn't be at my place, he landed in the best barn possible and is continuing his career with William Fox-Pitt in England.

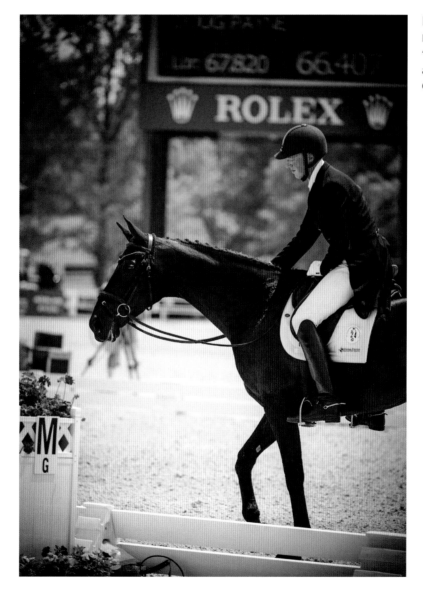

III.36 Doug on Running Order, his "horse of a lifetime," at the Rolex Kentucky CCI**** in 2012.

Acknowledgments

I consider myself incredibly lucky to have been born with some talent into a very supportive equestrian family with an uncommonly solid foundation anchored by my parents, Dick and Marilyn. They have been, and will always be, my barometer for success and the people I rely on most in my decision-making process. I would certainly not be where I am today without the opportunities and guidance they provided.

The truly incredible aspect of equestrian sport, which seems to separate it from many pursuits in life, is the community that fosters success. I can't possibly thank the countless people who have impacted my life, whether my riding, business, or academics. I'd be floundering without you.

Index

Page numbers in *italics* indicate illustrations.